STONE, PLASTER AND STARS

Suja Ravilla Ramana

Order this book online at www.trafford.com
or email orders@trafford.com

Most Trafford titles are also available at major online book retailers.

Printed in the United States of America.

ISBN: 978-1-4269-5315-6 (sc)
ISBN: 978-1-4269-5316-3 (hc)
ISBN: 978-1-4269-5317-0 (e)

Library of Congress Control Number: 2010919280

Trafford rev. 02/03/2011

 www.trafford.com

North America & international
toll-free: 1 888 232 4444 (USA & Canada)
phone: 250 383 6864 ♦ fax: 812 355 4082

For my grandparents

Prologue

This book is a little more than an attempt to share my colorful experience of studying dentistry and practising it. It's also a ringside view of the world from my particular corner of it. Little did I realize during my studies the extent to which it would define my identity or shape my destiny. Many of the events described here are real and some of the characters in the book were inspired from the dental world. The four years of studying dentistry and one year of internship was not nonstop entertainment. There were times when I had to work hard in the preclinical labs, clinics and study through the night. And then there were times when there was a joie de vivre in the air. It was the joy of feeling alive and secure as part of a family. It was the awareness that the journey of life had begun perhaps. There was much hope and enough ignorance. It was youth. It was heady and all encompassing.

Another vital influence during the period was the result of following Carl Sagan through 'cosmos' an epochal work that popularized science and got us to wonder about the origin and evolution of the cosmos and ourselves. About our 'pale blue dot, a mote of dust circling a humdrum star in the remotest corner of an obscure galaxy'. It endured over the decades in spite of all other attributes of the business of everyday living.

The decision to practice dentistry was however deliberate. It was the response to an internal wake up call that highlighted the importance of 'now'. Practising dentistry did not take me away from lofty matters as I feared it would initially. On the contrary it has been useful employment and lively enough if I include the multifarious quirks of people and only mildly stressful even if I included recalcitrant patients. Dentistry certainly does not have explanations for many matters which require one or why we feel pommeled about as we do sometimes but it has been respite as I ponder the points in the quiet of starlight. So much for dentistry.

Initiated

'the matter of the cosmos has come alive and aware'
Carl Sagan

My wisdom tooth had just been extracted. I was dazed though not in actual pain. It was a new experience in my seventeen years of life. Dr Pranay who removed it was one of my father's old buddies. They greeted each other heartily as only college mates can. He seemed the type who put people at ease effortlessly, he smiled as he spoke and even the grey glass and steel equipped operatory seemed cheerful. He helped me into the dental chair and examined the tooth. He suggested I have it removed as it was impacted and tilted towards the cheek, giving me a chronic cheek bite. When my father and I agreed he called out 'LA' to his assistant who handed him a syringe within a minute. He strode about with a flourish and gestured vivaciously but his fingers were gentle as he worked.

He started to inject into the gum around the tooth. He assured me that I would feel a small pain in the beginning and thereafter only heaviness. My eyes widened as I felt the local anesthetic infiltrate the tissue and a strange sensation flooded and froze up the area. Having an injection done is the only way you'll know what it feels like. But I was silent unwilling to draw attention to myself. About 2ml of the solution was deposited and the needle retracted without a single murmur of dissent.

"Good girl", he said, "now let's wait for the local anaesthetic to work and then we will pull the tooth out."

I nodded readily eager to be done with it. He got me talking, no doubt to take my mind off the impending procedure. Soon we were onto books and he was pleasantly surprised to find that I was familiar with authors he mentioned.

'Have you read Jane Eyre? he asked conversationally and probably expected just another nod. But I had much to say. It was one of my all time favorites and I even knew some paragraphs by heart. Nothing could stop me from gushing on, not even the heaviness of my sedated tongue. It must have been obvious to him that if he did not intervene soon the anaesthetic would wear off as I warbled on, even before he started. And there were other patients waiting outside. He closed my mouth gently and called his assistants.

They brought a steel tray set up with many heavy instruments and cotton. I tilted my head up and held it still against the headrest, listening to the rattle of instruments as steel clashed with steel. He put in a pointed instrument to loosen the cuff of the gum around the tooth. I did not protest, I could feel nothing. The LA was working. He held the tooth snugly with forceps and began to loosen it in an inward-outward swing. He disengaged it slowly from the surrounding gum tissue after a few minutes of traction. He examined the tooth, concentrating on the tips of the roots as he looked. He seemed pleased. The tooth had come clean without mishap.

I did not look at the tooth too closely. The whole idea still seemed rather gauche and I was finding it difficult to think neutrally. Before I could think of an intelligent comment to make he tucked gauze wrapped cotton over the empty socket and told me to close on it. An assistant called my father back into the operatory. Dr. Pranay held up the tooth for inspection. We stared at the unwanted ivory colored appendage that still trailed blood after it. It was a third molar, the so called 'wisdom tooth'. It would go into a bottle of hydrogen peroxide like it's predecessors to be claimed promptly by clinical students. They ensured that there was a perennial demand for extracted teeth as they scoured clinics for natural teeth. The tooth would be drilled according to the rules of 'cavity preparation' and filled. Later the root canals would be accessed, x-rayed and filled again. Students needed to wreck all the havoc they could on extracted teeth. How else could they learn to save those in the mouth? I did not know all this then of course but still felt a twinge of sadness as it fell with a dull clang.

Like all parents my father was worried more about my nutritional intake. He asked Dr. Pranay when I could eat my next meal, what I could eat etc. 'Bland diet' he replied even as he wrote out the prescription. We thanked him and were ready to leave surprised that a tooth extraction could be managed so pleasantly. He had also refused fees since my father and he were old NCC mates who had flown Tiger Moths together. 'No, he said firmly, restraining my father from taking out his wallet.

Earlier as I sat in the waiting room I had become anxious. My seat was opposite the operatory door and I could not help looking in whenever the door opened. Dr. Pranay and his assistants were busy around the patient. Instruments were handed across the drape and cotton rolled and tucked into the mouth. A suction tube was inserted to keep saliva from pooling. Instructions muffled by the mask he wore could still be heard. 'Stone' 'plaster' and' impression' was repeated but the one I had was, what a choice of career. They willingly put their fingers into someone else's mouth and thought nothing of it.

Just as we were about to leave he said impulsively, 'wait-a-minute' and reached across to a bookshelf nearby. He selected a book after going through a few volumes. He signed it and held it out to me. I felt genuine happiness welling up. This went way beyond being nice to an old friend's daughter. My cheek still felt as if a stone was taped over it and my tongue dry and sluggish but it was the *Oliver Twist* in my hands that made my eyes water. I managed only a weak 'thank you' though I was in raptures over it. I was criticized continually at home for 'extracurricular reading' instead of the prescribed text books. This book would not only validate my favorite occupation but also instantly elevate my status at home. I had grown up in the imaginary world of books and my head was full of phrases from them as I lived in a Utopian one of my own. The printed word never failed to fascinate me, except of course in the text book.

"If one has to be a doctor, then one has to be a doctor like him," I gushed to my sister as soon as I reached home and the blood stained cotton was out of my mouth. Before long I discovered that he had more fan following. My mother had worn an off white saree with the tricolour border that day and was greeted with "hello mother India, how are you!" She was flustered initially but smiling a little while later. She would also remember it for a long time but I doubt that he had the same impact on her, as on me. It was my first brush with dentistry and it remained firmly at the backburner of my mind.

Today in my practice I make it a point to give away little gifts to my patients, especially children. The crayons and the soft toys are a pleasant surprise for them but rarely do I give away books.

College

"nature has a four billion year head start"
Carl Sagan

I joined dental college two years later. I stayed away for the first few weeks hoping all the ragging would be over by then. Unable to postpone it any longer I sneaked into college midweek, crept up to the classroom and sat in the row before the last. I knew the last row attracted attention for all the wrong reasons, it was familiar territory after all. I avoided it as much as the front bench. I was neither studious nor disciplined and eyed the occupants of the front bench with great disdain. But I was not a classic backbencher either because I sometimes suffered from bouts of kindled conscience and put in sporadic effort. First day in college was almost over. The first hour was anatomy. The next was physiology and less intimidating. The practicals were in the afternoon and the last hour of the day was dental materials. After that I could go home, read my current book, stare at the night sky and eat. Or so I thought.

But the seniors heard that there was a new junior. They came in the evening, a motley group of a few boys and girls, curious and energetic enough to rag me, at the end of the day. Little did they know what they were up against. I was chubby, unfriendly, wary and hardly the type to play games with. I was sure that they would let me go after they asked me my name, the school I came from, my marks, why I wanted to be a dentist etc. The listless interrogation was almost over thanks to my unenthusiastic replies. But one girl in the group who sat on a desk at the back brooding over her maroon painted finger nails decided that they had not come over for nothing. She would rag me a little before sundown.

She told me to take out a page from a notebook. I fumbled with the zips of my huge knapsack as I tried to open it. The first thing I encountered was the large tiffin carrier in it. It was three storeys high. One contained *samba*r and rice, one *rasam* and rice and the last one curd and rice, in that order. Then there were two other smaller boxes, one for *poriyal* and one with *varuval* to accompany the main courses. The poriyal had grated coconut sprinkled over the boiled vegetable, to be eaten with sambar or curd rice. My mother instructed me to eat the varuval or fry with the rasam rice. She had also put in slices of salted raw mango in the curd rice as if the poriyal was not enough! I was mad at her as it crossed my mind though I had gobbled it all up at lunchtime without complaint. There was hardly any space left in my bag for the notebooks and the pencil box. I grew out of the pencil box within the first week in college but the water bottle soon occupied its place.

My mother had always refused to cut down on the lunch she packed and insisted that I finish all of it, everyday. Little wonder then that I weighed as much as I did. My sister probably shared most of it with friends. That must be the reason she was slender as a twig. Belated enlightenment I sighed as I pushed the towering edifice of embarrassment deeper into my bag. I was going to be the laughing stock of college if they saw all of it.

At last I found the notebook I sought at the bottom of the bag. They continued watching me as I tore out a sheet from it. I pointed it at the girl who asked for it. "Tear it into two," she said without taking it. I folded it in two and tore it at the crease. "Keep doing it," she instructed, "till I tell you to stop." I continued till it became a mere bit in my hand and difficult to hold, far less fold. Now she told me to roll it into a ball. I held it awkwardly between my round thumb and forefinger and rolled it into a misshapen little ball. I was at my wit's end and full of misgiving. What would she ask me to do next?

"Drop it" she said, which I did, thinking she must be out of her mind. If one year of dentistry could do that to a person I wondered what would happen after four years and the additional year of internship. But before I could say anything she gave me a little push and said, "Go play with the ball."

I stood staring at the ball completely clueless about how to manage the situation but definitely resentful. They waited for a while hoping I would start kicking and be a sport. I was no sport and I was close to tears. How could I play football with a tiny paper ball I could hardly see though I kicked myself sometimes when I was alone? My mind simply refused to consider the possibility of playing along or being ragged like this. I was not one for such casual games. Didn't they know I gazed at the night sky, was in communion with the stars, mused abstractedly (at nothing) and generally lived on a higher plane? I stood rooted to the spot, unable to speak, my tears willing them all out of sight.

We heard the college bus start. Smoke billowed from the exhaust and the engine made a racket no one could miss. 'Go' they said in one voice disappointed but unwilling to miss the bus to pickle a sourpuss like me. I picked up my heavy bag and ran heedless of the 'tzang' 'tzang' noises my lunch boxes made and jumped into the college bus. I felt genuine affection for the noisy bus. I hurriedly took off the coat I had forgotten about and as there was no place to sit, I stood trying to hold onto the overhead bar. I could barely reach it at my height and it was an effort just gripping it with dysfunctional fingertips which had not yet recovered from the attempted ragging like the rest of me.

My knapsack banged from left to right, every time Vardhan the college bus driver braked which seemed like most of the time. Did he think the speed breakers were specifically designed by the corporation of Madras to challenge a spirit like his? Vardhan continued to thwart them at every opportunity and I dropped the cotton coat twice on the girl next to me. She did not turn to look as

7

I gingerly picked it up from her lap but gave me an icy glare when she stood up to get down, a few stops before mine. I hoped she was a classmate and not a senior who would rag me later for this. Hardly in the mood to find out and resigned to the fates, I got down a little later glad to be home. What a day. I had just weathered a storm but acted nonchalant when my parents enquired about the first day in college. "Did anything sensational ever happen in a dental college?" I asked and watered it down to the subjects taught. I tried to sound thoroughly professional even slightly bored as if it was just another day. What was all the fuss about?

Initially the college bus seemed like a lifeline out of college especially after the futile ragging but soon I found faster ways of getting away which included anything on four wheels except motorized fish carts. There were two others who could not wait for the college bus which started it's circuitous route back at four in the evening. We formed the 'early club' when we met on the main road an hour earlier. Renitha was the undisputed leader of the club. Shahnaz and I were equally passionate about leaving early but less resourceful. We formulated rules for the club. The first was to ask for lifts only as a group. The second was to avoid vehicles with heavily tinted windows. And the third was to assess the combined strength of the occupants and climb in only if we were convinced we could take them on if needed. Flimsy reasoning and hardly fail proof but luckily it never got tested throughout our lift taking stint in college. We preferred open MUVs but then lift seekers can hardly afford to be choosy. We settled instead for vans or matadors or jeeps or cars, anything that stopped for us.

Our parents were horrified when they found out and warned us sternly about ever repeating the act. They told us to wait for the college bus or to come home by PTC. Pallavan transport corporation was state sponsored, untamed terror on the road and timings were least reliable of all surface transport by any yardstick. A standard joke during Pongal or New Year on every Tamil channel. The other deterrent was Vardhan's selection of audio tapes. He seemed to have quite a few crammed into the dashboard but 'chandirare, suriyare' was the only song we heard everyday. It used to be amusing in the beginning but was hardly tolerable as the weeks passed by.

College seemed more like a higher secondary school but without the uniform. There had to be more to it than just the academic curriculum spooned out to us. The curriculum itself was rather unimaginative I thought, with only anatomy, physiology and dental materials to complete the grind. There was no English literature or even another language to break the tedium.

Anatomy was taught by Dr. Santhi Karthikeyan. She was a mild mannered person, gentle, yet capable of a sharp comment. She always drew diagrams on the blackboard before starting the day's lecture. The attendant would bring in two chalk boxes before she entered the class. One box contained coloured chalk and the other white chalk. The class fell silent as she laid them out on the table. She started by drawing an outline profile of the face. An early indication that the anatomy of the head and neck would become our preoccupation. The profile was basic without a single unnecessary line. It was drawn with a steady hand and rarely did we see her use the eraser. I liked her sense of calm, the way she drew diagrams completely absorbed in them, the spell unbroken even as she turned around to pick up different colours of chalk. She coloured the veins blue, the arteries red and the nerves yellow. She spoke in a clear voice devoid of artifice. We sat up in class and jotted down notes. It was a pleasure to watch her teach.

We practised the profile on the blackboard till the strokes came easy hoping to impress her. Even those of us with two left thumbs kept at it till we could draw it reasonably well. Examiners correcting our papers would know we were her students. Many of them were probably her students too. If we were looking for a role model there she was right in front of us but I was too independent in my thinking already. I wanted to see the world, read more and figure it all out for myself. I was argumentative and disagreed with norms when I decided to speak. But I was generally morose, stark contrast to my younger sister who was cheerful and garrulous. She tried to shake me out of my melancholy and seemed to know how to make people laugh. Everyone except me.

I walked on the terrace pacing up and down with such an air of gravity that it could be easily mistaken for something important. I lay on my back watching wisps of clouds passing by, the colors of the sunset melt into each other, the sky darken, the stars come out and the moon as it weaved in and out of the clouds. I studied the hare on the moon. It found it riveting and stopped staring only when it went behind a cloud. Evening turned into night but I was in no mood to go downstairs and start my 'evening assignments', euphemism for homework in college. I would be more annoyed if there were guests or practical tests to prepare for, the room to tidy up or anything at all that kept me from going to the terrace. But for dinner I told myself I would stay on in the terrace, happy to sleep under the stars with a balmy breeze in attendance.

When I went up again the next day, I would start afresh with the silent sky. I never came to any conclusion at the end of it or even attempted to though it had become a compelling evening ritual. I was perfectly content to watch the spillover of moonlight and wind in benign collusion with the long leaves of the coconut tree leaning over the terrace. Perfectly content to smile back at the stars that seemed to shine benevolently at me, for me. Perfectly content to just 'be' in effortless harmony. A state of existence that can rarely be achieved when youth passes and cares have wormed their way into your mind.

Thus I failed to make Dr Santhi Karthikeyan my role model though I did give it some thought. I continued as sloppy as ever but became revengeful of attempts to discipline me at home. Yet I got by in college, even did well sometimes when I actually studied in a fit of guilt though I never distinguished myself in the subject. I was aided in this by a useful short term memory which helped me to remember the names of muscle groups, their origin and insertion, the arteries and their branches, the motor and sensory nerves and their distribution and hold it all in my head until the test was over. I promptly forgot all of it once the paper was submitted. But to my surprise Dr. Santhi Karthikeyan became fond of me, a favor I knew I did not merit. When she smiled at me encouragingly I was elated and even reconsidered the role model issue. I became a little more studious and even tried to answer questions in class. One of her favourite questions was, "What are pheremones?" I came home, asked my mother, wrote it down and memorized it. She was my ready reckoner and only too happy to enlighten me on the topic instead of the usual 'come down, start studying, oil your hair or pack your bag."

Physiology was fascinating. It opened my eyes to the functioning of the human body and the precision of enzymes that kept various metabolic processes catalyzed and regulated. I was amazed at the cascade of biochemical events that were triggered off as if on cue. How simple it seemed and yet strung together in such complexity.

Dr. Sharmila taught us biochemistry. She was young and a little anxious to make sure she got across to us. She also seemed to know that biochemistry was formidable. She made every effort to make it appear as if it was within reach. When she got married a few months later and left college, we missed her. She never thought any question too ridiculous to merit an answer.

Dental materials was a subject I took to unreservedly. Memorizing types of calcium hydroxide, kaolin, beeswax or carbonates of sodium or potassium or their percentage compositions may seem geeky but not for me. The librarian was an amicable fellow. All I had to do was ask about his daughter, a six month old toddler and he would even issue me reference books, as many as I could carry. I toyed with the idea of manufacturing dental materials. It seemed a far brighter idea than practising dentistry about which I sensed an insecurity. You studied anatomy but not all of it. You studied physiology but not all of it. Was I imagining it or did dentists sound rather defensive at times? I decided I would go into the more enterprising allied field of materials manufacture.

I started reading about the structural composition of different materials, about their transitional temperatures, physical states, stresses incorporated and energy liberated during processing, all with the ultimate aim of manufacturing them. Besides I had become ambitious. I wanted to make my million soon. I loved being on the terrace doing nothing and knew it was a luxury. How could it be sustained indefinitely without backup? Or could it be that one of my father's many sermons was working? He was a self made man who came up from scratch. My grandfather had been a freedom fighter in and out of jail before he passed away early. My father walked many miles to school and made it to college on scholarships fending for himself. He was now doing his PhD. I was convinced that if he could do so much with his background, I ought to do more with mine. But lethargy was also in my blood and I rarely acted upon such impulses.

My father refused to give up. He kept at me to improve myself worried that I would stagnate because of my laziness. He told me repeatedly that it would not do to just pass. He wanted me to excel. Why only academically, I screamed silently and sometimes loudly. Couldn't I make my mark on the world without A's in the dental subjects? I was not articulate enough to spout the classic line of teenagers, "it's my life", but that's what I felt as the terrace became my haunt. I was anti-establishment and now made it a point to question all accepted ways. I went so far as to say I was not going to practise dentistry because I was already training for it. The dental materials manufacture idea gelled in the meanwhile and helped me save my face. In my mind's eye I already saw many racks of freshly packed dental materials and an overfilled cash box nearby that would allow me to ruminate endlessly on the terrace.

I did not know that most dental materials were made by large corporations with massive infrastructure and years' worth of research. And I knew nothing of marketing or after sales. My parents must have known but did not try to talk me out of it. They thought it was a matter of time before my grand illusions cleared up and I stepped back to reality. But they were surprised at my interest in money for all my cosmic talk and outlook. At least I was interested in something, they solaced themselves reconciled to my lack of interest in the academic front. They hoped that the idea of manufacturing dental materials would keep me from becoming wayward. They concluded that my obsession with the terrace was perhaps deflecting me and tried to curtail the time I spent there. But no, I would not accept that, it was as essential to me as food and drink. I sulked and fretted and argued till they gave up.

In the classroom I stayed where I began, in the last row but one. I had always made fun of the first benchers and their enthusiastic ways, now how could I become one of them? "They are such enthu characters" I had proclaimed in condescending tones, ensuring my permanent stay at the back. However, this did not prevent me from writing "We are star children born of the universe and powered by the stuff that powers the sun" on my desk. This was after I began watching Cosmos by Carl Sagan. My view of life centered around the time I woke up, racing my sister for the best mangoes and improving my grades in order to avoid adverse comment underwent change.

Knowing about the origin of the universe and stars and planets and vast interstellar distances made light years seem like small currency. The fact that the unbelievably overextended cosmic outback was probably humming with life stirred me up. The deeper we navigated into the cosmos the more we would know about ourselves, our origin and our future. My walks on the terrace became imbued with meaning now. I was convinced that knowing was of paramount importance. It was the frontier to challenge, made easier because there were people like Carl Sagan to tell. He was one man with enough perspective. But was it possible to retain such stellar perspective in spite of the mundane daily routine? I was back at being the sulky teenager when I remembered the prosthetics practicals session the next day.

The class was split into batches for practicals that continued throughout the year. We put on stiffly starched white coats and brought out our trays from the locker. We fiddled with them as we waited for the instructor to start our first prosthetics practical session. The brand new prosthetics kit consisted of an extra large surgical tray with two plaster knives, two plaster spatulas, one bent and one straight, two green bowls which turned fluorescent within the month, two wax knives, two wax carvers and a McIntosh rubber sheet. We were told to spread the MacIntosh over the counter and then begin work so that the lab would be reclaimable for the next batch, after we were done. We also carried pencils and a scale. This was our basic armoury and the reason for most disputes. We made marks on instruments as on the McIntosh to prevent inadvertent exchange. Our instructors encouraged us knowing it was a matter of time anyway before instruments were exchanged or missing and pandemonium broke out. Once during a fight over a plaster knife one boy claimed 'it's mine' because it had 'mine' etched on it. Such was the rate of turnover of instruments. Rarely did we get to use the same instrument twice.

The first assignment was to make one inch cubes of plaster. We were taught to mix plaster and water in the right proportion and shape it up into a cube. Right proportion meant that the plaster mix should not be so runny that it ran off the slab before you could pull it up or so thick that it solidified in the bowl before you could coax it onto the slab for setting. The correctly matched water-powder ratio was the first tenet of the prosthetic laboratory. A scoop was used to measure out plaster and a small cup to measure water. "One cup water and two scoops of plaster" was announced many times during the session. Few of us got it right on the first day though we were busy as bees making unusable mixes. Soon there were great heaps of bizarrely shaped lumps of plaster piled by the sink. Many rivulets of watery plaster also ran into it but the masterpieces were those hidden under it. The sink was the final arena in our tryst with plaster. I doubted that the plaster would ever shape up into a cube given my inexpert manipulation.

First you had to measure water into the bowl and then add the plaster. You waited for the dumped plaster to settle down and then mixed it in with a spatula smoothening it against the sides of the bowl. Timing was everything. You should not be too fast or too slow but just vigorous enough to make the mix creamy. You had to make sure that there was no unmixed plaster that had somehow eluded the water. And finally you had to tap the bowl to bring up trapped air to the surface. Or else, we were told, you would get gaping holes in the cube because of air bubbles. I mixed the plaster into the water and started to tap the bowl on the counter as I had seen the instructor do. The instructor was Dr. Manimekalai who could make mincemeat of you if you were foolish enough to show her anything but a mix of the right consistency. When I finished tapping I was dismayed to find plaster missing from the bowl. It was all on my face.

I wiped it hastily on the sleeve of my coat before Dr. Manimekalai could see me. As I ran to get another measure of plaster and water I felt heaviness over my forehead. I put up a hand to check. It was plaster setting on my hair. It was warm because of the exothermic heat of the setting reaction I surmised brilliantly, remembering from theory. The plaster seemed to be everywhere. I looked like an apparition in white with semiset masses of plaster dangling down my forehead. It must have happened when I unthinkingly tucked away stray strands of hair loosened from my ponytail with plastery fingers. That would account for the state I was in. My hair was white and my hands were white too, up to the elbows. I tried to think about what to do next, though I was in pure misery. How was I going to get rid of all the plaster on my head and also have the mix ready when my turn came to show it? I did not know it then but dental plaster and dental stone would be the brand name on all our clothes and instruments for the next few years.

In the meanwhile I was mortified as I had a vision of Dr. Manimekalai taking me to the demonstration table, pointing at me with a straight spatula and saying, "This is what happens when you tap too much." I was seized with panic. I wished I had continued in the labour management course instead of dentistry. There were no practicals and I could have gone on and on about theories in economics or management hierarchy or work ethics. Where was my legendary calm? Had it all vanished because of a few lumps of plaster? Someone tapped me on the shoulder and I turned around fearfully expecting to see Dr. Manimekalai.

It was a pretty pert looking girl I had seen earlier in class. She sat in the middle row and spoke less. She held out a wad of wet cotton and motioned that I should use it to mop the plaster from my hair. I removed as much as I could the first time, wet the cotton and started again. I kept at it till my head was as light as before. The girl had gone back to her part of the counter. She continued making mixes and inverting it on the granite slab. She was calm and collected as if nothing unseemly had occurred. A little later she said softly, "Press the edges of your rubber bowl together before you tap it," cautioning me against making a spectacle of myself again and initiating me into the first unwritten rule of the prosthetic laboratory.

I thanked her mumbling on about timely help but she just nodded and went back to work. I watched her as she used the plaster knife to raise the walls of the cube at a sharp angle and then remove the excess. Were there more unwritten rules I did not know about? I thought she was industrious and hard working with nothing on her mind except the soon-to-be cubes she was making. Later I found out that her name was Esther and that plaster cubes were hardly on her mind. And that she was almost as lazy as me, in the same league anyway. We became great friends a few cubes later, were bosom pals before submission day and best friends by the end of the year.

Dr. Manimekalai told us to leave after a while probably thinking that we might use up all the plaster in the lab if allowed to stay long enough. She watched us as we filed out trying not to laugh. I could see her trying to link each ghastly cube to its' immortal sculptor who in turn hoped her memory was not as sharp as her tongue. Lunch hour in the staff room would be a long one. Esther had saved me from becoming prime time discussion though I was certain I would not escape Dr.Manimekalai for long. At least I was spared on the first day I sighed.

We made dozens of cubes hoping that at least a few of them would qualify finally. We bought different grits of emery paper and sandpaper to smoothen the sides of the roughly hewn cube. We started with a coarse grit like 60 or 80 and then went on to the finer oens. We were at the cubes till they were smooth and measured one inch on all sides. I threw away the worst and took the others home to use as paper weights. Nothing original about the idea as all the paperweights in college were one inch cubes that did not make the grade.

We discussed the cubes in great detail. We took them out one by one and admired or denounced them as the case was. We pointed out the flaws in each other's cubes and tried to shortlist four. Even tiny defects in the cubes could turn out to be major disasters at submission time. If it was a millimeter short on one side or there was a small pit defect, it would not do. We made more and more cubes in the never ending pursuit of the flawless cube. At last we had four that were almost perfect. We polished them gently with the finest grit of wet sandpaper and soaked them in soap water. We rubbed them with soft linen and cotton and gauze to get them shining white and translucent like no one else's. I wrapped my cubes in gauze and Esther hers in velvet. We tucked them snugly in sponge lined boxes as if they were precious jewels. Anyone listening to us talking near the locker would have indeed believed so. We expected to get A+s for our perfect cubes safe in their boxes. What could possibly go wrong now?

Just one day before submission Esther dropped a cube while looking it over one last time. I was still commiserating with her misfortune when I found that one of my cubes had slipped from the box into my bag and the pristine white was streaked a yellow brown. My cube was ruined because of the *rasam* that leaked from my lunch box. I came to a decision. No more three tiered tiffin carriers for me come what may. I would stand upside down rather than bring it again to college. My mother did not even try to conceal her amusement. Instead she tried to lull me into a false sense of complacency that I could make a better cube than the one I lost to rasam. But my mind was made up. I chose a small sleek oval shaped box and stuck to it throughout the college years. However I did not lose much weight as I made up for it at dinner and on weekends. Besides my craving for mangoes was undiminished.

Esther and I would wear the white coat as soon as we got down from the college bus in the morning. We took it off just before we got back into the bus in the evening. My taste in clothes was not sophisticated and I usually chose abrupt dramatic colors like dark maroon or deep blue. Suddenly I would sober down to pale pastels for a few days before another mood and a corresponding color overtook me. I was the typical teenager with shifting tastes and an unpredictable style. The coat was thus a convenient mantle to hide the clothes and the extra fat. Esther on the other hand had much better taste in clothes besides being thin. I wondered why she also wore the coat like second skin. The clothes I wore at home were worse. They were faded cottons of an indecisive shape with the stains of many mango filled summer holidays. I always grabbed the biggest mango from the spread on the straw as soon as I woke up in the morning before my sister could reach for it. My mother begged me to eat breakfast first as if I was going to fast. I would agree if it was *poori* or *upma* but refused *idlis*.

I started on the mango leisurely. Whatever the variety I would first feel it in my hand, turn it around and press it in till it was soft. I bit it at the lower narrow end of the fruit careful to make the opening

18

small. You could enlarge it later if required but if it became big the juice ran down your elbows and you had to lick it up if you didn't want to waste the nectar. I kept at it till there was no flesh left on the stone and it was fit to be planted in the ground for the next crop. I did the same at Chidambaram my grandparents' place.

When all the grandchildren were gathered for the summer holidays my grandfather fed us all from one plate. My grandmother would hand him a large plate, ladle out rice and curry and add a dollop of ghee in it. He delicately mixed it in with lanky time worn fingers that unconsciously added more to the generous sized balls of rice. Affection. He put it into our outstretched hands or directly into the mouth, depending on the age and dexterity of the kid. There were finer traditions in the family had I cared to look but relishing food required no effort at all and seemed like a lovely pastime.

I loved freedom, truth, the wind in my hair and starry nights. I thought a lot. I believed myself to be a soul that wanted to rise above itself. Then why was I lazy I asked myself given a cosmic agenda that included changing the world. Could nothing move me into action? I tried to overcome the inertia but failed repeatedly. My mother was a moderate person. She spoke to me about the middle path and cautioned me against swerving to the extremes. I doubted that all matters could be sorted out so simply and interrupted her even as she spoke. She had been young once and therefore perhaps tolerated my rashness believing it to be a passing phase.

Arihant, Antony and I were in one batch. Arihant was a quick brain but politically incorrect. He resented the mindless succession of cubes we had to make and aired his views loudly. I 'sshhed' him whenever Dr. Manimekalai was on rounds. He wanted to get on to the more advanced exercises. He thought it was kid-stuff mixing plaster and water all day and sandpapering cubes in the evening. I however felt that the dental materials department was justified in expecting us to submit four perfect cubes. Besides I got so used to making cubes that it was now second nature. I felt no urge to do anything else.

Antony was more diplomatic. He had mastered the art of making a little effort seem like much and was polite and soft spoken. But he became Dr. Manimekalai's favorite for another reason. He was the only one in class who could make a cube with less than two scoops of plaster. His detractors called out 'plaster saver' whenever he passed by hoping he would stop with less than two scoops.

Esther and I sat together during the bus ride home. We talked and talked. Our batchmates, seniors, professors, the dean, none of them were spared our critical eye. In the beginning Esther tried to refrain from judging people as she had been instructed to at home but the option was eventually ruled out. Still her noncommittal attitude prevented her from denouncing anyone outright or praising them too much. I had no such qualms. Actually I believed it to be a virtue. It was in the family. My father was outspoken and an orator. He could discourse on any one of his favorite topics namely politics, spirituality, feeding the birds or 'the curious neighbour' indefinitely. My mother was his constant audience during the variously inspired speeches. She was a good listener and encouraged people to talk, though he hardly needed any to begin. Sometimes I listened and sometimes I did not, to prove that I had independent ideas about everything including politics and spirituality. Esther and I discussed the origin of religion, worship and rituals, class struggle, the ills that plagued society, the role of science in bettering lives, movies, pop charts and the incurable Malayalee accent. We discussed dentists, their skill, their behaviour and tried to analyze whether the two were linked. Dental subjects came up only rarely during our unending arguments. But we agreed that pharmacology was fun.

Dr. Vani taught us pharmacology. She tolerated most of the stories we wrote good naturedly. She did not read them out in class. We remembered the drug dosages but made up almost everything else especially adverse reactions to drugs. Nausea, fever, malaise, vomiting, diarrhea or anorexia could be caused by any drug and many drugs did. We invented other side effects to drugs that were more fiction than fact but could not be proved completely wrong. Fever of unknown origin was a topic that interested me greatly.

Could the simple fever be caused by such a wide array of diseases / disorders?

Microbiology was free for all. Dr. Sivagnanam taught microbiology. She was gregarious though old and a little hard of hearing. She taught us about cocci and bacilli. And about other little creatures that seemed lifesize under the microscope and the mischief they caused but were invisible to the naked eye. She wrote on the blackboard mumbling to herself and waited patiently for us to copy it down. The girls giggled as if drugged with nitrous oxide but acted studious when she turned around to look. They hid their faces behind the pages they turned in notebooks. The notes were not downloaded from the latest BMJ but they were substantive from the exam point of view. Dr. Sivagnanam was completely removed from the college student mentality though and seemed more like a grandmother who had wandered into the campus. I liked the holiday atmosphere when she entered the class and was sad to see her leave.

The boys threw well directed arrows and accurately aimed paper rockets. The usual recipients were girls who seemed to be listening attentively and sometimes the microbiologist herself. Harini was one of the permanent targets of the boys. She sat in the first row and tied her hair in tight plaits which caught the arrows and held them there. She also wore thick glasses with dark horn rims like mothers'- in-law from the seventies' movies. She knew the boys laughed behind her back but stuck to her glasses steadfastly. Harini would interrupt the lecturer many times and say,

"Ma'am, could you repeat it again?"

That irritated the boys more than her spectacles. They were always in a hurry for class to be over and this explained the target practice with arrows. One day however they crossed their limit. Harini found seven stuck in her plaits. She began to cry and Dr. Sivagnanam became angry with the boys. She caught them red handed and marched the missile toting ones to the dean's office.

Another time she was too angry to speak and walked out of the class.

Harini was spirited. She continued to volunteer for bharathanatyam dance during college functions and to sing in music competitions. Whether she was trying to clarify a point in physiology or cracking a joke she was wholesome entertainment. She loved her curd rice and there seemed to be an unknown ingredient in it that brought out the best in her during lunch. Even those who kept reading or writing gave up the pretense of not listening and burst out laughing. I was one of her avid fans.

Pathology was taught by Dr Rajeshwaran. He was a thorough professional. He wanted to get the subject through to us, make us sound in basics and prevent us from committing any major faux pas. In theory or viva. I even bought the "big" Robbins instead of the 'baby" Robbins. Not Esther though. She stuck to the baby. My first seminar in pathology was 'factors which influence wound healing' for which I was allotted twenty minutes. I prepared for it in earnest. The entire college would be there and I had no wish to make myself conspicuous by talking nonsense or forgetting lines. I went to the library and gathered all the books I could find on wound healing. I compiled a list of the factors which influenced it. I divided them into systemic and local factors and began to study each one in detail. I timed myself using a 'two- in- one' and played it back to check for mistakes. I tried to anticipate relevant questions and prepared answers. I was the last speaker for the day. It was a saturday and the bus left early, at one. I hoped nobody would be in a mood to ask questions. It was almost lunchtime.

Renitha spoke before me. She spoke and spoke. She was hardly reticent in class but I had not expected her to be such an exemplary story teller. I had less than fifteen minutes to sum up my effort of the past three weeks. When I began the audience was polite contrary to what I expected. They did not boo me out. I quickly said all that I had to say. They clapped. I thought they were relieved I had not crossed my time limit. I ran to the bus to ask Esther how it went. She was my first sounding board though never forthcoming unless pressed for an opinion. Why did some people find speaking their mind so difficult? "You should be prepared to clarify doubts on wound healing. It is exam portion after all", she said. Did that mean it was Ok? It must have been. I was no authority on wound healing but if I had managed to sound like one then I was good at fooling people. I was actually unmotivated and my enthusiasm died the moment the grand words were out of my mouth. Overall however the seminar made me confident. I was sought out after that to speak whenever there were not enough contestants for debates.

Second year was a lark. Dentistry did not seem to be such a bad idea after all, especially after the pathology seminar. The disinterest I evinced about all matters dental was becoming milder. 'I don't know what I want but I want it now' would summarize my tantrums but they were leveling off. It is not to be assumed that I had turned over a new leaf and began studying. The concept of dentistry was amusing enough, to be taken seriously at times but certainly not all the time. Life was for living I told myself and what were the dental subjects teaching us? They taught us to bypass life. I could envision an ideal life without stress or discord and one in which results were exponential to the input. But where was the time, I lamented, with endless assignments to submit and tests to prepare for. I worried less about the loss of biodiversity and pollution than I did about my leisure time which had dwindled to zero. I was a typically confused and resentful teenager. A seething mass of hormones trying to reach their balanced state and as it happens most of the time, the mass doesn't know it.

I mused on abstractedly and thought about love. How it happened. If it was preordained and irrevocable why did it seem so fragile? There were a few couples in college who were always seen together. I observed them to see if I could solve the mystery but in vain. They seemed equally at sea and worse, unable to help themselves. Novels and movies had enough stories based on love but which one was to be taken as golden standard? How did one judge in such matters? I was certain this was just the tip of the iceberg I knew nothing about. I saw how preoccupied these couples were with each other but what stunned me was that they were so sure of themselves. Where did they find the courage to take life into their young hands and fashion it as they chose. Could it be as simple as it seemed?

I did believe in love. In an ideal and all consuming love that united two souls so completely that there was no ambiguity or selfishness. It was worth the while waiting for such a love, such a life. But how would teenagers know. Or anyone else for that matter. Yet they seemed certain as they looked into each other's eyes all day. I was sure my eyes would water after a few seconds, I could barely tolerate sunshine on a cloudy day. I knew instinctively that I lacked such insight and therefore acted as if it did not really matter. I spoke instead about making my million, about making it big and plans for the future. Besides it was obvious even to a novice like me that domestication was the end result of love. My mother spoke about love and marriage in the same breath and I could feel fetters when I heard the word marriage. Freedom was precious. I distanced myself from the subject.

Reading was my favorite hobby and I read more. I read quiz books to improve my general knowledge. I read how de Beers cornered the diamond trade and about the tributaries of the Amazon. I would blurt out 'Tylophora asthmatica' if woken up and asked to name the herb used to treat asthma. I read Bharathi, Wordsworth and Shelly. I memorized the Greek alphabet and verses from the *Tirukural*. It is remarkable that even then I was not driven to my textbooks.

I had long talks with my mother. I spoke to her about what I read and about the future. Sensing some of my inadequacies she would say 'there is something special about everyone. It is invisible to the others but obvious to the right person and will be recognized by a kindred soul'. My mother was sensible yet her eyes misted over when she spoke of love. She knew the uplifting power of love. My mother's family was idealistic. They fasted for soldiers during the Indo-China war and if someone had spoken of love, at least no one would have scoffed. They were closely knit as a family and knew about each other's emotional life. My mother was conscientious and lively. But she became thoughtful when she spoke about the attachment and passion that could be between a man and a woman, about the importance of the family and standing up for people, especially during a crisis.

My father believed in hard work and saving for the rainy day. For him the sky was falling, if it had not already. He cared for my mother deeply but was busy building up securities. Love might rhyme with cotton candy for him. It was sweet, colorful and seemed like a lot but did not weigh much in the final analysis. Overall I admired my parents. My mother managed her teaching job in college, chores at home, cooking, the two of us to raise, my father's lectures and grievances, all with the air of dutiful wife hardly concerned about herself. 'He worries enough for all of us' she would laugh. I was not one to fall into this well I told myself. I wanted to keep my options open. I wanted to be free and independent. I wanted to make my million soon and lead life on my terms. "Love," I quoted, "flew out of the window when poverty came in through the door." I wanted to travel. I wanted to see the world. But I needed money for it.

My father would never part with hard earned money just to satisfy my curiosity or because I got another idea. He was unfailingly thrifty and it was impossible to loosen his fist for trivial matters. Once convinced however he would spare the amount but the cause had to be risk free, proven and worthy. Considering the odds, I felt it was far easier to earn my own money. This worried them more than my laziness. What if I became wild and went out of the fold? Ours was a traditional home, a little conservative, though not stiflingly so. My parents wanted me to finish UG and get married. I would do nothing of the sort I promised myself. I would do PG instead. Now that we knew what the study of each speciality entailed many of my batchmates were already deciding on the subject for postgraduation. You could restore teeth, realign them, remove them or replace them though ultimately clinical work would be a little bit of each.

Oral surgery was not for me I decided with odd hours to keep and the stress of dealing with traumatic injuries and tumors.

Conservative dentistry was rather confining a field with fillings and root canals to do. Was that not narrowing your scope a bit?

Prosthodontics was too much lab work. Forget airconditioning, the ceiling fan had to be switched off at times to keep the Bunsen burner on and the molten wax could give you a sharp sting if you were not careful.

Periodontia did not seem broad enough with only the gums and bone around the teeth to think about. Was the study of crevicular fluid there enough to sustain life for three years?

Pedodontia was out of question. I was terrified of small kids. What about big kids, adolescents? If I were anything to go by better stay away from them.

Orthodontia was the subject I loved to hate. I would beg on the streets rather than become an orthodontist I told myself.

That left me with oral medicine. You did not have to slog in the labs, there was minimum physical work involved and it was definitely more theory than practical work. Suited me. I was a study in contradiction. I spoke about moving heaven and earth but when it came to doing it I did not mind postponing it. After much deliberation I went to the library. I looked up Burkit in the oral medicine section. It was as large as an updated Webster and intimidated by the size I put it back on the shelf. I picked up the less intimidating Basker and put it back on the shelf too once I made sure everyone knew I was interested in oral medicine. As for the other subjects I hardly cared about them until tests were announced and sometimes not even then. But I did my practical work and was on time with the assignments because I did not want to be reprimanded in front of the class. Both notoriety and fame were troublesome. Maintaining a low profile was the low stress, right way to live.

Dr. Roopa Rani was our orthodontia lecturer. She had a no-nonsense air about her and spoke sparingly. When it was Ortho OP we had to be on time and know about the appliance indicated for the case. She was brief and her instructions clear. You could leave once you finished your work. There was no need to hang around in the department or spout any new spangled orthodontic theories. That was the impression we got. I detested Ortho but was drawn to it initially because of her. One exercise that broke my back was wire straightening. We had to cut three inch long, 16 gauge wires from a roll and straighten it. The passing test was rolling them on the glass slab to see if they adapted absolutely against it. Many of my batchmates did it as a matter of course and stood in line to get it approved by Dr. Roopa Rani. Not me.

The wire rolled in my hands instead of the glass slab. Every time I gripped it with the orthodontic plier, it would slip. Thinking it was the sweat on my palms I wiped my hands on the long white coat I wore and started again. I almost nipped my fingertips off but the wires were nowhere near straight. How was I going to manage the next exercises in Ortho if the first one was so disastrous? We had to make clasps, finger springs and labial bows with a thinner gauge wire of course but still no cake walk. Then there was the coffin spring to make, the last one in the series. It was going to be my funeral I thought morosely.

Antony's father was an orthodontist and he seemed to have inherited the knack for it. I threw away the dented wires I had and got him to straighten out three new lengths for me. I bribed him with the *muruku* my mother made. The usually reticent Antony became less inhibited with help after that though I would not be persuaded to part with any portion of lunch. I patted myself on the back about the way I had solved the orthodontic wire problem but told no one else. I was sure it was nothing to be proud of. But at least I tried, I consoled myself and felt little guilt about subletting the exercise.

While the girls struggled with theory and practicals the boys had fun. They found the time to turn pages in text books just to look at pictures especially beyond the head and neck but the girls crammed and crammed unimaginatively, going chapterwise. All the Chaurasia volume III books in the library were dog eared because even in the final year someone could shoot 'name the muscles that constitute the floor of the mouth' at you. There was one boy in our class who wanted to be an oral surgeon and also the dean's protégé. He dressed like the dean, spoke like him, and was never seen without a Kruger. He looked preoccupied, as if he was mentally tracing the course of the mandibular nerve or the classic triad of a syndrome just out in the Lancet. We were amused but said nothing. He was getting bossy with the juniors but he was his usual self with us so we had no reason to complain.

When the workload increased Esther and I acted as if it we were not really affected by the college routine. We were two of the apathetic creatures we had identified as reasonably regular to college but the very act of 'being' tired us out. We let our bodies carry on metabolic functions. That was all we could do. We would use our brains for anything but dentistry. We acted as if it were an act beneath us, as if only the less developed of the species would take it seriously and not highly evolved specimens like us. Yet before exams we were invariably a sight. We slogged as if for dear life, so eager were we to get it over with. Imagine being stuck with it all a second time. That was our sole motivation to study. Knowledge for knowledge's sake? Ha! We would rather memorize the railway train schedule or countries and their currencies or capitals.

We wanted to go home as early as we could and were forced to take the PTC bus sometimes when we could not get a lift. Strangers leaned on us as the bus lurched forward or halted suddenly. We were furious and glared at them in reproach. We said 'excuse me' loudly so that others would hear and stepped on their toes if that did not work. Another observation we made was that middle aged men seemed worse than young boys in this aspect. Would having a boyfriend help at such times? We concluded that it was too risky. What if they became troublemakers too instead of troubleshooters?

Third year was no breeze. The subjects were general medicine, general surgery and oral pathology. Community dentistry was the only antidote to it all. General medicine was taught by Dr. Manivannan who was academic in outlook. Naturally he was strict. He did not like students who sat about in pairs or looked fashionable. Girls ought to wear nothing more stylish than salwar suits or sarees and boys conservative shirts and trousers. He wanted us to remember that we were future doctors and be meritorious. This outlook hardly endeared him to the boys. He was nicknamed '*Manni*', 'forgive me' in Tamil and avoided diligently, as he wanted to talk to parents too. This was college after all, not school. But I was not going to be the one to remind him and was careful with him in class and in the bus. I took off the oversized sun-glasses that kept me from squinting in the afternoon glare and hid it in my bag till he got down at his stop. What if he thought it was too stylish? Failing in medicine meant Davidson and Hutchison in tow for the next six months. The glare seemed definitely preferable to burning midnight oil with the hefty books.

Once you began studying you realized how vast medicine was. You hypothesized based on signs and symptoms, the history of illness, results of lab tests and finally arrived at the diagnosis. All to determine the cause of the patient's suffering. The more cases you treated, more rapidly did your clinical acumen get honed. But I was unable to see a case as a case. I worried about the patient becoming embarrassed or hurt. I avoided probing if the instructor was not looking, thinking I was being noble. I assured myself that I could manage the lapse with my glib tongue or the names of syndromes I seemed to have a knack for.

General surgery was taught by Dr. Craig Chacko. We looked forward to his classes because of the clarity with which he addressed each topic. We got the outline of the essay questions and could easily manage five points for short notes if we were attentive. He wore steel rimmed glasses that only partially sheathed the penetrating eyes, was a busy surgeon and acted like one. He spared us the drudgery of studying entire chapters of Bailey and Love. He sifted chalk from cheese and marked essential points that would help us pass. He made us revise them at the end of the lecture. We had to tell one point each, row by row. No one felt victimized, everyone wanted to remember one point that would take the question to the next bench. Even the chronic backbenchers tried to have a point ready for their turn.

Without being verbose, by just doing his job well, he managed to raise standards. He praised no one, belittled no one and seemed far above to get involved with kids like us. He also drove fast and obliged anyone who asked him for a lift. He taught well, practised well and seemed to be a content man. I think there were fewer frustrated people then. Competition was not annihilating. Bailey and Love became one of the well thumbed books in the library because everybody wanted to impress Craig Chacko. The boys tried to imitate him and the girls thought, so what if we are girls, we can still try.

Oral pathology was taught by Dr. Mohini Sivaraman. She was doe eyed and had long hair always in the ubiquitous single braid. She was an intellectual firebrand yet conservative in outlook. She was a lovely blend of east and west. She knew her subject well and knew that she knew. She could dictate notes for an hour or longer without once referring to books. She was thorough and would always follow a pattern about every topic. She started with the etiology and incidence, went on to the clinical features, histopathology, radiological findings and always ended with management of the lesion. And she had guts. I was certain it came from an indepth knowledge of the subject.

Community dentistry felt like an add-on right from the beginning. It seemed like a little bit of this and that in dentistry with the idea of a community thrown in. We went on a survey to a village off Poonamalee wondering how relevant public health could be to us. It was our first field trip and Vardhan played his usual *'chandirare'* song but we hardly noticed this time. We were excited about the outing. We had questionnaires to fill, pastes to distribute and data to compile at the community camp.

We had to speak to small groups teaching them the right brushing technique and warning them against the use of tobacco and *gutka*. We did it enthusiastically in the beginning but as the day wore on we became less vocal. When we asked 'how many times do you brush, do you use toothpaste or do you chew on the stick?' we found that roughly half of them used a brush and the other half used a natural twig . It may seem outlandish to those who're used to the toothbrush but many people in rural India still use the neem, babul and other natural twigs to clean their teeth. Some of them knew which extracts to use as mouthwashes. Not surprising since about 6000 plants in India are used as herbal remedies by local populations. One thing was certain, no one brushed again at night. The pattern became clear to me. I did not have to interview more people to fill up the remaining questionnaires. I could do it myself and the statistics would not be far from the truth. Actually I believed statistics were lies. The others had come to the same conclusion too and were busy cooking up data.

Most of the villagers were courteous and some even offered us coffee but we were glad when it was done. We entered a house, the last one in the row and the last one for the day. It was mid afternoon and sunlight streamed in through the window. A young girl was sitting on the floor, her back to the door. She held an oval mirror in her hand. There was a Cuticura talc by her side, a *saandu* container for her to apply the red bindi on her forehead and a bottle of coconut oil beside it. Her mother was combing her oiled hair, taking the knots out of the tresses before plaiting it. The girl turned around when she heard us enter and we instantly recognized Bell's palsy. Dr. Manivannan had succeeded after all. Because of facial nerve paralysis her eye would not close on one side. There was loss of facial symmetry as other orofacial muscles were also paralysed. Saliva drooled out of her lip on the affected side.

The house, the girl's condition, her preoccupation with her appearance, her family's acceptance of it, everything saddened me. I was angry too. Even the smell of the pleasant Cuticura became overwhelming. I wanted to leave. This was the beginning of real clinical exposure. Later we saw benign growths like lipomas and other cancers of the head and neck. Many malignant tumours seemed to have guarded to poor prognosis in spite of the options of surgery and chemotherapy or radiotherapy. There were also other infectious diseases and genetic disorders we had to diagnose. Initially we were filled with a morbid fascination but soon learned to distance ourselves by being objective about it. Still it was difficult to get over the horror of debilitating disease in an otherwise healthy individual. More incredible was the time lapsed before some patients decided to seek medical advice. Quite often the reason was economic constraint though sometimes it was the attitude of 'perhaps it will go away by itself' or worse still, 'it's my fate'.

There was the case of a benign but large growth on the neck of a young man in his early twenties. It had grown so big that he could barely turn his neck anymore on that side. He required surgery urgently as the growth was beginning to compress vital structures. He was told to get admitted immediately. I discussed it with Esther. We talked about illiteracy, superstitious beliefs, the human predicament and how people were trapped in it as we watched kids of the construction labourers roaming about the college campus and playing in the mud. Their parents worked at the site, offloading cement and bricks from the lorries and then carrying them up to the construction areas.

"We could have been one of them," Esther said though it was usually me who threw the bait. 'Why not?' I said. Why do things happen as they do? Who decides constancy and variability, change, the rate of change? I usually posed such rhetorical questions to impress her. But Esther would promptly say that 'it was predestined', or 'the intended way - it is so, because it is so.' Can you add much to that. I knew there was more, much more of cosmic proportion and it seemed to be a noble pursuit – the quest for truth and understanding. But it was also disheartening to realize that nothing was as absolute as it seemed. If time, space and reality itself was relative then where do you begin? I was glad I could voice these doubts to Esther during the lunchbreak. She would leisurely brush the crumbs off her dress as she gave it thought. 'Mmmm. Good question, she would say, 'but hardly urgent, hey, did you finish your perio assignment for tomorrow?'. I was on firm ground again, back to matters more relevant to teeth.

I was just another teenager in the rites of passage. In pedodontia we studied about the differenlt stages of childhood. I think I was stranded in the abstract intellectual stage before progressing to adulthood. But it was hard to believe that what I thought was the result of a bunch of hormones cruising along in my blood. I thought I was far superior, pondering the stars as Carl Sagan did. College, clinics, keeping up theory, examining and treating patients was full time occupation but I still found the time to wander on the terrace at night, to watch the stars and stare into the night sky. It had become a biologic necessity though I was not spirited enough to do more than wonder at the mystery of the universe and contemplate space odysseys from where I sat. It gave my everyday reality an unexpected perspective. It confirmed to me that my troubles were too trivial and worrying about my grades unnecessary.

Suddenly one day Esther was engaged. She would be married shortly. I felt a vacuum, especially after she started taking leave in preparation for the arranged marriage. I acted as if I took it in my stride but fooled no one. My walks on the terrace became longer and I became moodier than ever. If only I was more like my sister, even tempered and requiring no prodding to study. 'What are we going to do with you?' was uttered helplessly whenever my parents saw me lazing around, doing nothing. How long was I going to mope? Esther came back to college. She seemed sensible still and even argued like before but had changed anyway. She was a distracted young bride and seemed engrossed with her husband, in-laws and house keeping. My attitude was standoffish. Neither would I ask questions about her new life nor offer her anything more than a cold shoulder for comfort.

Esther was the rational analyzing type. She did not deplore me for my lack of insight or insensitivity on the subject. Instead I got wild once when she did not collect my handout from the prosthetics department. "Why," I demanded, were things changed so much now that she did not even notice I was on leave? Had her household chores and cares become so important ? I was miffed that she did not take my outburst seriously. She tried to stifle her amusement and be tolerant as if it was a teenage tantrum and I needed to grow up. A bigger crime in my eyes. Her nonchalance was something I had always admired but not then.

I sat near the window in the library reading the newspaper and novels I smuggled in or just looking out. I wandered around the campus feeling lonely and out of sorts. I even lost interest in the manufacture of dental materials, my pet subject. Once while passing by the table tennis court, I met Srilekha my senior by one year. She was feeling out of sorts too but I had no idea about what. We started playing and got along well. She appeared to be the innocent type in her modestly worn saree, long plaited hair and rimless glasses but was as eager as me to cut classes.

One day we gathered enough courage to go to the movies. For weeks we plotted and planned the details. We went to college as usual on that day, attended a couple of lectures and met near the table tennis court at the agreed time. We chatted for a while waiting for the bus but when PTC failed us yet again we stopped a car and asked for a lift. We got down a short distance from the theatre. We did not want our benefactor to know that we were truant college students going to the movies. We bought popcorn and peanuts, chomped on without a care, tossing the husks behind us as we walked. We bought iced orange juice from the roadside vendor which my father had expressly forbidden me from drinking.

After the movie we reached the bus depot by another vehicle and dissected it in detail as we waited for our respective buses to go home. We were in no mood to go back to college. The outing was successful but the movie was a flop. We must have been one of the few who had seen it during its brief run in the theatre. My mother had evening classes so she had given me a key with which I let myself in after the rendezvous. I did not like going back to an empty house though I sought privacy when everyone was home. A few movies later I lost interest in the escapades. With no one to stop us the adventure lost it's charm. Srilekha sensed it and suggested diplomatically that we had better study too. When I told my mother later about it she was surprised but seemed to accept it since it was over and done with.

It was my turn to be surprised. I expected to be scolded and warned in serious tones about 'consequences'. I don't think my father heard about it because he would hardly treat the matter so lightly. He not only called a spade a spade and a rascal one but also many other names. Another trait I inherited from him was coining names. Especially for people I did not like. They were simple codes but difficult to crack because it was part English part Tamil and part Telugu.

The batches were reshuffled. No longer did the A's and B's sit together. There had been a simple camaraderie amongst us earlier but the group feeling was reduced considerably after the medicine and surgery postings. We began to exhibit more independence as latent individuality and preferences surfaced. Group activities like plaster block preparation were no longer among our exercises. We made occlusal rims from wax sheets and set acrylic teeth in them and acrylized it fabricating the complete denture. True you needed skill and could ruin someone's denture if you shifted the midline even by a millimeter but it hardly seemed to matter when the fellow had *ascites* or a *motor neuron lesion*. But we did not dare tell our lecturers that. We started needing more working space, more elbow space and finally more breathing space. It was not long before we acted as if we would rather be on our own. Yet we needed bonding at times and our discussions could be very practical and there was always more to tell Esther whenever I saw her.

I studied hard during the exams. There were days when I studied through the night till five in the morning and then found that I had only two hours to revise it all before I ran to the bus stop. Of course, I wished I had studied right from the beginning but it was only a passing thought. I did not want to waste even a minute on the eve of the examination. I crammed and crammed. Till the invigilators told us to put away our books and we were let into the exam hall. I came back and slept like the dead. It was late in the evening when I started studying for the next exam. I studied till all the essay questions I had marked important were completed. Then came the short notes.

I usually spent more time finding out the important questions than studying portions in the syllabus. I collected previous question papers and tagged them date wise. I made a tick for essay questions and a cross for short notes, marking it every time it was repeated. Thus the most important questions had the most number of ticks or crosses. When I prepared for theory I always started with the question that had the most number of ticks or crosses. Most people including examiners follow a set pattern and rarely divert from it. So more often than not

I was right. News spread about the accuracy of my guessing and I became the one to consult during last minute preparation. In spite of it I could not relax till I had scanned the question paper cursorily to be sure I knew at least fifty percent of it.

I wrote steadily, in a confident hand. I didn't believe in scribbling, even if I did not know the answer. I thought the examiners would get irritated trying to decipher it and then finding out that it was nonsense. Neither did I believe in antics in the exam hall. If the naughty ones asked for answers I would whisper a key word that would help them spin a story for a short note, no more. I did not pass my paper around for others to copy. What if there were mistakes in it? Exams were dreaded but once I started writing, I got into the act and did my best. I tried to sound as unambiguous as possible though Esther said I was expert in the art of sidestepping.

I drew nice pictures, nothing original just colorful reproductions from a hazy memory. I shaded them in misty hues especially where my memory was faulty. It was a carryover from geography at school and it seemed to work well in college too. I surpassed myself in drawing curvaceous mandibles. Fractures of the mandible and its management was an essay question and anyone reading about it in my answer paper would think I was the one to seek should they unfortunately break their jaw. Even the examiner could have mistaken me for a budding oral surgeon. Actually the best I could do was to refer them to Dr. Murugesan my teacher of oral surgery.

Answering in viva was more complicated, actually the first step in PR management an essential aspect of medical or dental practice. The examiners thought you were fit to pass if the damage you would do was within acceptable limits. After all everyone learned by experience including doctors. It was the internal examiner's job to make out what else was on the external's mind. They would concentrate on looking non-commital as if they wanted justice to prevail but later came out during the tea break and leaked the external's favorite questions. Fluorides were the backbone of dentistry and examiners could go into any detail on the topic and most of them did. The sources, the ideal levels, the biomechanics of absorption, mechanism of action, insufficiency, overdose, everything about fluorides was important.

By the time we came to the final year we were not greenhorns any more. You had to have enough common sense to be polite whether you we knew the answer or not. You had to wait till they told you to sit. You should not grab the chair in spite of feeling faint or nauseous as the examiner's favorite topic was one you had neglected to study. It took more composure if you knew the answer and were turning mental cartwheels with joy. You must look as if you were carefully considering the question because if you jumped up eagerly to answer the next question would be tougher. The most important thing however was to look them straight in the eye. You had to speak crisply and to the point. You should not imply that you know more even if the topic was your alloted project work. You had to wait for the question like a well trained dog awaiting the next bone hopefully but without being too obvious.

If the going was good and you were ultimately caught with a question you knew nothing about then you should smile politely and say "sorry sir, I don't know." They'll let you off with a pass. Most of the externals were just decent guys who wanted to make sure that you were not clueless before you left college. Viva skills were gleaned from years of performance analysis during impromptu get-togethers. It was the most common topic for discussion before and after exams. Each one tried to describe their experience humorously but always after the results were announced. Almost all of us had an interesting story to tell especially if the examiner was a sport. Most were, though we liked to imagine them as hungry barracudas with many rows of teeth. The internals were important too, the only tangible link between the external and the word 'pass'.

I went in for the prosthetics viva prepared for anything but the first question. "When did you last wash your coat?" It was almost yellow now at the end of four years of dentistry but I never felt the need to buy a new white coat. I had passed each year with the same coat and was determined that I should wear it for the final exam too. My head was stuffed with removable partial dentures, fixed partial dentures and complete dentures. The brain area to manage a little tease like this was frozen. My mouth went dry and not even a cackle or croak would emerge from it. The internal was bright. He realized that I had developed a tongue tie.

Before I fainted, he said, "she washes it sparingly to keep luck from getting washed off." The external smiled and the viva went on smoothly enough after that. He must have thought I was a drip, no point trying any friendly mocking. I got through. Wasn't that enough? As soon as I came out the remaining members of the batch rushed out to ask me how it went.

"What is his favourite topic?

"Is he strict?

"Does he expect the exact word or is he a little flexible?"

Antony was always the first guinea pig. The defense he had developed over time was smiling. He smiled and smiled trying to charm the examiners even if it went badly. He continued smiling even as we quizzed him, when he came out. 'Speak up' we hissed trying to psyche ourselves up.

There was one boy Yugesh who took the cake when it came to the viva. He was the official class jester and it was no coincidence that this should happen to him. External examiners are pampered beyond belief. There were plates of cookies, dry fruit, cut fresh fruit, wafers and bottles of 'cool' drinks on the table. And there were 'specimens'. A partially edentulous mandible, a pathology section in a formalin jar or a packet of sodium fluoride with the concentration etched out of sight. They let you pick up whichever you liked and proceeded to grill you on it till you regretted your decision.

When Yugesh entered for his viva, the external a strict lady on the right side of fifty gestured at the pile expecting him to pick up one. His eyes were drawn instead to the goodies in front of him. He had the audacity to think she was asking him to help himself to the cookies on the table and said

"No thank you."

"No? Come on, pick up one,"

she said pointing at the dental specimens, hoping he would look away from the *samosas* and *pudina* sauce nearby. Not Yugesh. He replied shyly a second time,

"No, thank you" thinking she was offering him the wafers this time.

The external burst out laughing and the atmosphere turned festive. This became one of the iconic batch jokes and Yugesh was asked to repeat it on stage at every college function. He had a sweet temper and none of the lecturers who threatened to detain him kept up their promise. His marks were usually in single digits but he kept his cool. If he was detained he appeared again for the exam cheerfully and continued with the jokes.

I had become complacent during my pedodontia viva and soon fell from grace. It was the eruption sequence of permanent teeth. I started well but mucked it up towards the end. The dean and the pedodontist who had told us to be thorough with the table tried not to look judgemental. I had true affection for the printed word but when it came to tables I could be knocked down with a feather for all my weight. I had seen the table both in Finn and McDonald but could not bring myself to memorize it. I was paying for it now. The "hang me if you must " look would not do. They just might. I tried to look brave instead and the examiner changed the topic. After I answered the next question they let me out.

Passed.

The dean was livid as if I had let him down personally. He caught me slouching towards the college bus head cast down and asked "Are you planning to become one of the permanent fixtures in college?" I had nothing to say, second time in the day. But from then on I called him tiger Thiagarajan because he pounced on me thus. Later the equation changed when he found that whatever my lapses in the dental field I was one of the few in college who could continue the poems he recited. "All the world's a stage" by Shakespeare was one of his favourites. I took out my English poetry book from school and memorized the poem afresh. I continued reciting even when he paused for effect. At least it was more fun cramming compared to the eruption sequence of teeth.

The dean was a good surgeon. I had seen him extracting teeth as if he was demonstrating a trick. He smoked a lot and his fingers trembled sometimes but he knew his job. Most dentists confine themselves to the study of the head and neck and more specifically the teeth. He was not happy about it. 'Dentists think it's unclean below the waist', he grudged. He wanted us to study more. He wanted us to think and act like general surgeons. It was hard enough memorizing the various muscle groups in the head and neck, their blood supply and nerve supply, even with the help of mnemonics. Who would willingly inflict more on themselves? The ones who thought differently got the gold medals of course.

Sagar and Kalpana were the pair of our class. We called them hero and heroine and looked out for them in the morning. They usually wore matching colours. If Kalpana was in a black saree Sagar would be in black too and on the days she wore pink or yellow he would wear a pink or yellow shirt too. The color coding seemed rather cinematic but the point escaped them completely.

Sagar looked deeply content and Kalpana glowing and bubbly as they got off the bus in the morning. The rest of us were ready to slink back home if we could. Vardhan still played the '*Chandirare*' song but they hardly noticed so engrossed were they with each other. They spoke on the phone for hours in the evening, no doubt about the color code too and continued the next day in college. We wondered what else they talked about but were too bashful to ask. Sagar was also a practical joker and while the rest of us agreed he was not upto Yugesh's level Kalpana found every one of his jokes hilarious. She would laugh and blush so much that she was red in the face most of the time. They were usually seen together at all times except during Dr. Manivannan's class. He nodded his head in disapproval, this could not but diminish the time they allotted to the study of medicine. I considered myself a mature soul. I could see from the old doctor's point of view as well as the young doctors'.

I watched them at lunchtime. Kalpana was studious and wrote notes for both of them. Sagar sat by her chair chatting and looking for excuses to sit there longer. He looked directly into her eyes as he ate spoonsful from her tiffin box. Kalpana brought rice, roti, idli, or noodles for lunch. Sagar ate most of it whatever it was. Kalpana was flustered. She tried to keep up conversation about the recipe, how it turned out last time or some such thing but hardly ate anything. Something else was keeping her alive, not food. Sagar in the meanwhile continued gazing at her as he ate, his head angled on his palm. It was as if he was trying to memorize all the features of her face lest he forgot a line or curve.

Kalpana had eyes that talked or laughed. They were a deep black with equally dark and long curling eyelashes. She lined her eyes with *kajal* everyday in addition to the elaborate *bindi* on her forehead. On the day she decorated her hands with *mehendi*, she would stretch them out to Sagar. Did he like the pattern? It was obvious whom she dressed up for. Sagar's eyes lit up and his languid drawl turned energetic when he replied. In the evening he looked wistful and could hardly let go of her bangled hand when she got into the bus.

The girls giggled uncontrollably when they saw them but the boys were jealous. And since Sagar was possessive of Kalpana he got into minor scuffles with some of them. I wondered how they managed college work with so much to distract them. And yes they had their share of fights too, a reminder that the temporary suspension of ego in the throes of love could easily be revoked sooner or later. Sagar would look sullen and angry and Kalpana tearful and unhappy. They did not wear matching colors on those days and would hardly turn in each other's direction. It usually did not last more than a few days when they got over it. And then it was back to motorcycle rides and chocolates. They married while still in college. A few others in our class got married too and we were all into our own lives. College matters were not top priority any longer.

43

Clinics

"every star may be a sun to someone"
Carl Sagan

Dr Jansi Inian's clinic was on the first floor of the commercial complex a hop skip and jump from home. The first thing that struck you about the place was the aroma of food. There was an eatery downstairs that sold *bajji, vada, pakoda,* and *bondas.* The piping hot stuff was served on a banana leaf or stitched *badam* leaves with coconut chutney. I tasted everything sold there except brinjal bajjis. I did not like brinjal because it became unbecomingly soft after cooking. It got under my skin. I learnt it was called aubergine in French but detested it anyway though it sounded more suave than in English. My mother would tell me to get a parcel when she did not have time to prepare a snack for visitors. I would take the brinjal bajji home if I did not like them.

I was just highly opinionated but thought I had a nose for people. I expressed my likes and dislikes openly. I could not be persuaded to come down from my perch on the terrace and speak to guests if I did not want to. My parents made excuses for me. They said I was studying or sleeping at that time but admonished me later for being unsocial. I talked for hours with people I liked and that was hardly unsocial, I pointed out but to no avail. You had to entertain people whether you liked them or not and being choosy was a luxury few could afford.

Dr Jansi was enthusiastic. You could see she had a lot on her mind but came to the clinic with a spring in her step. She would ask Leela about a chore at home or the kids' meal or about the instruments' sterilization even as she entered. Leela was her woman Friday and assisted the doctor at home and in the clinic. Dr. Jansi would talk to patients in a frank and matter-of-fact style that left no room for doubt. I suppose it happens when you have raised three children and always need to make the score clear. This was the first private clinic I was attending and was proud that I went to meet Dr Jansi on my own, introduced myself and got the job. She agreed to let me assist her after college in the evening.

She was working on a patient as I sauntered in at half past six the next day. She was excavating a cavity on a lower molar. It was quite deep and she would probably put in a temporary filling. Being the new assistant I decided to get the filling ready. I turned towards Leela who had assumed I was there to usurp her post. I asked her where the temporary was and she gave me a look that squeaked, "Can't you see I am busy" as she rattled instruments. I ran back to Dr. Jansi and asked her. She pointed her finger in the direction of the lab and told me to relax. "It's not an emergency and I have to excavate some more," she said smiling. I went back subdued and waited till Leela handed me the glass slab and the cement spatula giving me the 'here, mix it if you must' look.

She had piled a little mound of zinc oxide cement at one end and added a drop of eugenol nearby to mix it in. Now I wished I had watched the cement mixing demonstration in college carefully and not from the back of the crowd. And I had never waited long enough to see it set having retreated early since I was conveniently at the back. What had gotten into me today, why was I acting uncharacteristically enthusiastic? I thought for a while and concluded that it was the bunch of *agarbathis* lit in a corner. I was intolerant to strong smells and usually avoided close smelling places. But how could I object when I had just joined half an hour ago?

Leela gave me a look that clearly indicated that she had been in practice long before I joined dental college. I looked away and started mixing the cement powder and liquid trying not to breathe in too much of the agarbathi as it smoked in incessant waves. The mix seemed a little dry so I added a drop of liquid. Now it was too thin so I added a little more powder. It became too thick so I added another drop of liquid. Finally when I thought I had the right consistency the mix was the size of a small lemon! I was afraid to even look up. A grain sized mix was all that was needed and I had mixed enough to fill all the teeth in the patient's mouth. Leela gave me a stare of disbelief but said nothing. Perhaps if she were not looking I could have hidden some of it in the pocket of my coat but she would not take her eyes off the slab. She probably expected me to be axed the same day.

Dr Jansi was mercifully still excavating. She called out once to ask for the two way syringe. I ran across, handed it to her and came back to the glass slab. The mix had grown to the size of an orange. If Leela was annoyed with me thinking I was competition, she must have stopped worrying and started pitying me. I was an uninitiated nervous wreck. I was looking at the mix from different angles wondering how I could make it shrink when the doctor motioned to me to bring it over. I scraped a pinch of the cement off the glass slab and held it out to her at the tip of a filling instrument. She had the cavity excavated and irrigated and dried. It was ready to receive the temporary. If she noticed the trembling in my fingers she did not mention it. She began adapting the cement into the prepared tooth. She shaped it up and smoothened the surface. After she checked the bite, she put in a small roll of cotton and told the patient to close his mouth. He was dispatched with instructions to come two weeks later and not to bite anything for the next half an hour.

Dr. Jansi turned towards me a half smile already forming on her lips but froze midway when she saw how much cement I had mixed. She tried to compose herself and said after a moment, "You have mixed enough cement to plaster all the cracks in the wall." I

46

had expected to be reprimanded even more severely. I apologized and looked so thoroughly shamefaced that she relented after a while. 'It's ok', she said, 'you are learning still.' I looked crestfallen but Leela was not content. She seemed to think I ought to be spanked for what I had done. She got her day's share from the doctor for putting an instrument that had fallen down back on the tray. Was mine a lesser crime? Before she could comment however another patient came in and we became busy.

I felt tired and beaten blue and black. I berated myself for suddenly turning enthusiastic without prior practice. When I reached home I acted as if I could tolerate no more for the day. My parents refrained from asking 'how was the first day' thinking the cause of my tiredness was the increased workload. Not my sister though, she wanted to hear all about it.

"Come on, start, what happened today?" she demanded even as I raised up the volume of vividh bharti and acted as if I could not hear her. I settled down with a book thinking if I appeared engrossed in it she would stop. Studying was always top priority in our house. She snatched the book from my hand, turned down the volume and asked me again about my first day at the clinic. My expression was one of impatience. Silly of her to suspect that something could go wrong.

"It was fine," I said. I think my voice gave me away.

"Come on," she repeated, "what happened, did you just get scolded or are you fired?"

Good grief! did she guess how close she was to the truth? I pulled the blanket over my head and pretended to sleep.

A few days later Leela and I were on talking terms. Once she realized I was too inexperienced to be any real threat to her job she became friendly. She liked the doctor but it was tough for her, she grumbled, assisting at home, in the clinic and managing the doctor's three children. Leela had joined the doctor twelve years ago and was almost family as she helped bring up the children since they were tiny tots.

She was the prime source of amusement for me in the clinic apart from the occasional fussy patient who made us twitch with laughter. Though she was uneducated, Leela tried to use as many English words as possible in each sentence. It was the pronunciation as much as the vocabulary that made my hair stand on end. But I was wary of offending her and promised myself that I could laugh later at home. She was seemingly curt and short tempered but actually kind at heart. She had no particular feelings about anything except her employer's children whom she insisted did not have enough manners. She was content with her job.

I watched the doctor as she did fillings, extractions and root canals. As I assisted I would try to correlate what I studied with what I observed clinically. Sometimes I would make out a feeble link but most of the times I could not. You read about microscopic enamel prisms and dentinal tubules in the textbooks but all you saw in the mouth was a dark hole in the tooth. You could see the orifices of the root canals but you could be certain of their definitive outline only after checking with x-rays. I did not bother the doctor with my observations. Neither did she bother me with questions about the composition of cements or the eruption sequence of teeth. She was content to let me assist silently especially since I wasted acceptable amounts of cement of late.

College had become synonymous with questions and more questions shot at us by lecturers and seemed like a thorn in the side. Just when I decided clinic was definitely less taxing Dr. Jansi had to leave town. She told me to take care of the clinic for a week. Could she be serious? I had passed the final exams, was doing my internship and wrote doctor before my name but considered myself a kid still. I told her I could not do it. College was different, there were lecturers around all the time. But she would not take 'no' for an answer. "You can" she insisted, "once you get started you will be fine." She gave me the contact numbers of another dentist who would come by, should the necessity arise. I had no choice but to do it. Otherwise she would think I was ungrateful and rude. I finally agreed thinking all I had to do was to keep the seat warm for Dr. Jansi's friend till she came. I would call her every evening.

I became responsible overnight. I was in a rush to reach the clinic. I went early and sat huffpuffing for a while. I became fidgety and doubted the wisdom of the whole idea anew especially since Dr. Jansi's friend had left town on an emergency. I considered running back home and would probably have but for the patient who blocked the doorway. The young man walked in complaining of toothache. Leela seated him on the dental chair and I examined him. He had a grossly decayed molar which was extremely painful. There was a small swelling but no pus discharge. I prescribed an antibiotic and an anti-inflammatory pain killer and told him to come for extraction two days later.

I had done it! I had seen a patient by myself and made a decision about his tooth. I was practising dentistry. Contrary to my expectations I felt professional and satisfied. Soon there was a family of four, one screaming kid included. I was overwhelmed. What if the kid was the patient? Perhaps I had been rejoicing too early. They told me it was a courtesy call and that none of them were patients. They had come over to visit Dr. Jansi socially. I offered to get them Mysore bondas with a special potato and carrot filling, so relieved was I. They refused it but wanted me to inform the doctor about the visit. I promised them I would and they left a little while later the kid still bawling.

There were two more patients later in the evening, one for a filling and another for extraction. The filling was for a cavity on a premolar and went without a hitch. I excavated the decayed tooth as much as I dared with a hand excavator. It was deep so I avoided the drill. What if I exposed the pulp? I based it with calcium hydroxide and filled it with glass ionomer cement. It was biocompatible, released fluoride and did not stand out of the tooth like silver fillings. It could be called the poor man's composite. I smoothened it with a polishing bur.

The tooth to be extracted was loose in its mooring. It ought not to worry me. But it was my first extraction outside college. And this was not the oral surgery department where lecturers leaned over the other side of the dental chair to make sure you angled your syringe right or to ensure that you had the right grip for traction. This was a private clinic and I was responsible for the patient. Beads of perspiration formed on my forehead and ran down my neck and back. I was soaked to the skin before Leela loaded the syringe. The patient might survive the extraction but would I? Leela sensed my anxiety and became supportive instead of the mild sarcasm she usually displayed. She handed me the syringe loaded with anaesthetic solution for the injection, nodding encouragement. It was the standard 2% lignocaine with a little adrenalin in it. I took it from her and held it up for inspection.

I tapped it a couple of times gravely, cinematically, though there were no air bubbles in it. Unable to postpone it any longer I bent down to inject it, my attitude grim. I worried about all the things that could go wrong, ranging from simple syncope to shock. I was all alertness as I started injecting without batting an eyelid. I told the patient to keep his eyes open so I could check his pupils. I was extracting a premolar in the upper jaw. I deposited the solution slowly on either side of the tooth. I withdrew the needle gently as if from the grey matter of the brain. I informed the old man that I would wait till it got absorbed into the area. The patient was almost toothless. He probably had many extractions done earlier but listened to me meekly enough and agreed. I went to the sterilizer to pick up the extraction forceps. It slipped from my hand. I dived sideways and caught it just before it hit the floor. It was very hot and I rubbed my scalded palms together as I waited for it to reach room temperature.

The cotton was wrapped in gauze and the prescription written down. Only the tooth remained to be taken out. I prayed for the roots to come through without breaking. I had seen it happen in college and knew it was messy business. Retrieving the root tips took time and effort, even if you knew how to do it. And I did not, at least not without expert guidance. I curbed the downhill direction of my thoughts summoning enough courage to begin. Further delay would make me nonfunctional from anxiety. A long and unwanted list of complications was already forming in my mind with numbered bullets. I gripped the tooth with the beaks of the forceps. I twisted it in the socket till it was almost disengaged. I took a deep breath and pulled the tooth out in one final wrench. I put it down reverently on the tray. The extraction was done without any complication unless I collapsed on the patient. The patient himself was quiet and relaxed.

I showed him the tooth hardly able to keep a minor sense of triumph out of my voice. The old man was only mildly interested. There was minimal bleeding and I tucked cotton into the site of extraction and gave him postoperative instructions. I recited most of what our lecturers said in oral surgery OP and the patient left after he paid the fees. I sighed as I sat down. The adrenalin was in the local anaesthetic I had given the patient, then why was my heart beating so fast? At this rate I would probably not last beyond a dozen extractions. I had enough excitement for one evening I decided and looked up at the clock. It was nine. I made a list of the day's patients, the amount collected and stood up to leave.

I gave Leela a benign and mature smile and thanked her for her help. She grudged me a look of mild admiration. Mixing cements and handing over appropriate instruments was one thing. Doing it all on your own when your chief was away was another. I was pleased with myself and was a changed person by the time I reached home. I was happy. And wordy enough to call my sister for a chat. I wanted an audience. Unaccustomed to such courtesy she became instantly suspicious of my motive and wondered aloud whether I wanted an exchange of her new blue dress. We held periodic exchanges of watches, hair bands and dresses. The one who called for the exchange usually benefited from the deal so you had to act as if you didn't need it and bargain harder.

I smiled a slow smile as if my new station in life was far above such minor considerations. My sudden benevolence took her by surprise and she ran to tell my parents that something had indeed happened to me. My parents were only too pleased to see that I had become responsible at last and dependable. I had proved myself. My sister was however uncomfortable with my newly ennobled outlook as she did not know how to tackle the makeover or how long it would last.

Dr. Jansi came back a week later. She appreciated me for managing the clinic when I handed over the money in an envelope with the daywise list of patients. I was again content to mix the cements and write out prescriptions. I was also back to my original brooding self and started going late to clinic and coming back early. So much for my enterprising makeover. After a few months Dr. Jansi's clinic was closed as she shifted it to a place near her residence. I went to work in Dr. Prasannakumar's clinic nearer home. He insisted on paying me for assisting him. I should have been happy about the arrangement but was not. Now I had to be regular, punctual and manufacture credible watertight excuses for taking leave.

Arihant my batchmate in college also came to the clinic as his father and Dr. Prasannakumar were friends. In the beginning we stayed away from the front desk and also from patients as we acclimatized to the new place. We poured models in the lab continuing to make the mess we made in college. We made silly dolls with the excess stone. We carved our initials out of the stone that remained after the dolls. There were dozens of A's and R's and S's and other alphabets stacked in the cupboard depending on the names of the assistants. I had assumed the initials were my idea but realized all the assistants did it. How deeply a person's name is etched in his psyche!

We gossiped, did the fetching and carrying required of assistants and even held babies when the mothers needed extraction. We did dental work only when all the three chairs were occupied. The doctor was not a taskmaster. He was lenient and talkative. The patients were all treated to a smile first, a relevant hot topic discussed and then asked about the dental complaint. He had the knack of making people unwind and relax. He liked to socialize and it showed in the evening OP. Yet he was shrewd in his own way.

Sometimes before a patient came in, he would predict exactly what the man would say. He grinned at us as it was repeated verbatim. We laughed when we got the drift of it but stayed out of discussions when it got deep. I found it stark contrast to the college where we were expected to maintain silence at all times. The only noise in the OP would be the muted clang of instruments as they were placed on the tray and trying to be inconspicuous had become a habit. You could afford to breathe noisily and let people know you were in a particular corner if you knew the answers. Most of the times I did not and learnt to breathe silently. My ego did not need accommodation in the OP and I could survive even if I was not praised.

One of our principal duties in the clinic was to usher the patients in and seat them on the dental chairs in the operatory. Next we found out whether it was an extraction or filling or a denture. If it was an extraction we loaded the anaesthetic in the syringe and brought the forceps. If it was a filling we brought the filling instruments and mixed the cement. If it was a denture we got the impression trays ready. We made numbered tokens from brown cardboard and kept it in a box by the door. The patients would pick them up in the order they came in and then sat down to wait for their turn. They became impatient sometimes and contradicted each other. Once we had written out two sevens instead of one and both the patients pushed at the door righteously displaying their tokens. The doctor laughed it off, pacified them and asked them to sit down and wait side by side.

There were other 'regulars' who came to the clinic but not as patients. One was an income tax consultant of forty five. He was unmarried and brought photos of prospective brides every time he came. He would say his mother insisted that he marry the girl in the photograph and describe all the features of the girl including those not visible in it. He would enumerate all aspects of the alliance - the good, the bad and the unnecessary. He had three or four gold colored pens stuck in the pocket of his safari suit and strutted about talking in a loud voice even as the doctor worked. He thought he had the audience in thrall and kept up the one sided conversation with only an occasional 'hmmm' from the doctor to show that he was listening. He would leave late in the night only to return a few days later with another photograph.

Arihant had no patience for small talk. He wanted to learn to work independently and learn fast. He wanted to start a clinic soon. It was his father's idea that he should work with the doctor to pick up practical points. He was reluctant but came anyway because he did not want to displease his father who was funding the new clinic. Arihant did not like the doctor's style and would sometimes comment adversely about a treatment option or the way it was executed. Soon enough, the doctor sensed it and preferred me with certain patients. Dr Prasannakumar also told Arihant's father not to buy new furniture for the proposed clinic. He suggested that he could start with unwanted stuff at home and buy new furniture as his income increased. Arihant was furious and stopped coming to the clinic. Another girl Monica joined within a week. She was also focused about her career and was looking for a place to start her clinic. I had such examples before me but it never struck me to think of starting a clinic. Instead, whenever I found time I would wander into the garden.

There was a fragrant *nagalingam* tree by the wall and when the moon rose over it's height moonbeams encircled it like benevolent fingers. I was spellbound by the silver shine that silhouetted the curling flowers adorning the branches. Even the watering can and broom became objects of enchantment as moonlight imbued them with great depth and ethereal beauty. It was paradise that would vanish with the click of an electric switch or the 'szzzchh , szzzchh' of the broom from the neighbour's yard. My core, just the essence unaffected by everyday experiences or my half hearted attempts at being worldly wise surfaced. I felt unfettered and free. It was freedom from all restraints, overt, subtle or imagined. I felt elevated into the cosmic realm even if only briefly like a tentative little pulse on a steep waterfall. Difficult to sense the depths but you try to imagine it anyway.

Consciously we live on a plane which includes needs and duties but rising to a higher plane like this makes living worthwhile I told myself. At such times I thought of love with a clarity that was lacking at other times. What we want in love I would decipher in a flash of revelation was what you expect of yourself. Nothing less, if not more. Someone who could address issues boldly even if there were no clear answers, feel on a similar scale and on the same tantalizing wavelength creating harmony. This would set the pulses racing, make eyes speak to each other and hearts to beat in accord. DNA reaching out to DNA. Was it just chemistry ?

My parents were proud that I got through college and was doing my internship. No matter how much we try to prove that we are answerable to no one else's wish but our own it is a deep source of contentment to see your parents proud of you. I was the first doctor in the family unless one of my ancestors, unknown to me, had squeezed juices of herbs on wounds and healed sick people. My parents had started looking for a match for me. They were not interested in my starting a clinic. They reasoned that I had to locate my work where 'he' lived. I protested when I came to know of their efforts. I always protested whenever they came up with a plan for me and not myself.

A year later they wanted me to meet a young man who was doing postgraduation in neurosurgery. For what? I asked suspiciously. Oh, socially, at a friend's place, they replied but I was not convinced. When my mother bought me a new saree to wear for the occasion I knew something was brewing. I sensed that it was a proposal of marriage.

"How can you humiliate me so? I yelled vehemently angry. It seemed so primitive to be decked out in finery and paraded before others. To be assessed and approved of or disapproved of.

"I will never agree to it," I screamed and kicked a bamboo chair nearby to reiterate my point. It had always been in the way anyway. My mother realized the gravity of the situation and sat down to talk to me on the terrace. She held my hand and promised me that nothing would be done against my wishes. It was all up to me and I could decide whether to proceed with the proposal or not to. All I had to do was to meet a new family, have the snacks and coffee certain to be served there and be back home within the hour. "Would it not be rude to refuse in the last minute?" she asked in conciliatory tones persuading me to go along.

Later in the day I was face to face with a serious looking young man his spectacles positioned precariously on his nose. He kept slipping them back on and glancing at his watch as if he was in a hurry. He was on duty at the hospital he said as if in explanation and then proceeded with the questions. He asked me my name. He asked me where I studied. He wanted to know which speciality of dentistry I was interested in and what my hobbies were. I replied to all the questions in monosyllables trying to fathom what else was in his mind. I did not succeed. Neither could I come up with penetrating questions that would help me decide either way. It was time to leave and I was certain that was the end of it.

It was the beginning. Venkat called up the next day and everyday after that. He had decided to marry me and was actually talking about a date. "No," I said clearly. It was too fast and too early. I had not yet made up my mind about him or even getting married. And then the chocolates and the flowers began to arrive. My parents were amused and my sister giggled nonstop but I was not ready to give in yet. I agreed to meet him again but only to find out why he wanted to marry me. "Love," he replied matter-of-factly as if asked to state the obvious. "Infatuation," I insisted, certain that the meetings did not correlate with any of my preformed theories on love. I suggested he think hard and long before making such a major decision. I also told him that I was lazy and prone to tantrums to help him decide.

Venkat was in no mood to listen. Instead he flooded the house with greeting cards and books and more flowers. My sister said I was being unnecessarily cold but my parents appreciated my caution. He called many times daily and would not pay heed to my advice of `go slow'. Eventually I relented and was caught up in the whirlwind too. I agreed to marry him. Besides marriage seemed far less strenuous than starting a clinic or even working in one. Later of course I realized the folly of my assumption but did not know it then. Based on the period of engagement I thought marriage would be a continuation of leisurely dinners, moonlit beach walks, misty morning walks and soul to soul talk. We were married two months later. I believed him when he said he would always be there. A fundamental miscalculation. I should have asked "where?" because he was always in the hospital.

Crossroads

"there may be many other universes"
Carl Sagan

I joined the hospital too after completion of internship. The dental OP was the last one in the block or the first depending on how you looked at it. The head nurse's office was to the right after the registrar's and across was the dispensary. I liked the location of the dental OP. It was airy spacious and well lit. Two sets of windows increased the sense of roominess. So what if the curtains were held in place by IV tubing and there were holes in the cloth? You got a good view of the diagnostic center and college of nursing and physiotherapy.

I watched as ward boys, sweepers, students, nurses, patients and doctors walked in and out of the newly renovated gate. It was the only ornamental piece of metal painted in recent years. The rest reminded you of radioactive decay. It was the trees that brought the buildings to life. I left for the OP at about 10'o clock turning off the radio. It was usually tuned to Madras FM and I would hum along creating the only disharmony in the song. I considered it a sacrifice when I switched it off before leaving. Dr. Acharyulu was the senior dental consultant. A relaxed man in his mid fifties his approach to dentistry might at best be described as a mild one. When I joined I had expected to see many patients lined up and a busy doctor unable to cope. I thought I would assist, which I generally preferred, to being in charge.

But 'no' Dr. Acharyulu said, "It's always a lean period from October to February." "Besides," he offered as further explanation, "they have raised charges recently, for extractions and fillings."

I had always been one to escape work but now I wanted to work in order to justify my salary, the meager allowance I drew monthly. I wished we would get busy. It was getting boring staring at the diagnostic center. Usually there were medical representatives waiting outside the door. No one else could make a doctor feel like one especially when there were no patients. "Doctor, please," they would plead, "prescribe this analgesic for instant relief from pain" or "prescribe this antibiotic for excellent infection control." "We need your extended support and cooperation regarding this product" etc and would leave you with samples in a neat pile on the table.

Sometimes other doctors passing by would walk in to greet me. They stayed to chat for a while. I wondered that they found the time to bother about an insignificant addition to the health mill like me. I discovered the reason soon enough. The sisters treated junior doctors like spoilt children who would take offence at the slightest provocation but had to be taught patiently anyway. They barely tolerated them hoping they would not get too much in the way. No wonder then that the miffed junior doctors circulated more outside their departments. It was only the heads of departments who had sisters running after them during rounds. Chiefs had a lot on their minds. There were patients who needed surgery, attendants who needed explanations and emergency cases to be posted immediately throwing the existing theatre schedule into disarray. And a neglected wife and irate family members.

Getting married itself was an altered state of existence and if the doctor you married was doing postgraduation life became a fast spinning wheel with the axis gone haywire. Words like rest and normalcy had to be deleted from your vocabulary. I realized I had been prepared for the prototype of the relaxed man who would provide as a matter of course, comfort and converse. I had assumed that talking to me as we sat on overstuffed armchairs would be his principal occupation. I was vaguely aware that he had to go to work during the day but expected he would be home at all other times. What I found instead was that Venkat was almost always in the hospital. His timings were incredible. He came home at three in the afternoon or at three in the morning. And when he came he ate quickly so that he could leave as fast as he could preferably without uttering a word. It transpired that he did not believe in small talk.

I also found that I had to cook, pack, clean, wash, scrub and sound uncomplaining as well, whenever we met. Even more surprising was the fact that he expected to be fussed over whenever he remembered to come home to the postgraduate quarter. Was he behaving like a married man who knew his wife too had a job in addition to the responsibility of running a home, I asked him. In the meanwhile I had to reassure my parents and sister that everything was the same as before, nothing that mattered had changed!

Sometimes he asked me why I looked so strained. Before I could begin from the long list, he would say, 'I am doing postgraduation after all!' I was furious. I thought I should do postgraduation too just to improve his perspective. But I toned down and refrained from airing such views. He might actually ask me to start studying for the entrance exam. Not speaking my mind was however unnatural to me, used as I was to endless discussions at home. But I realized before long that it was futile trying to argue with him. He would assume I was warming up for a fight and that this was the prelude.

In the beginning I got up early, cleaned the house, put in the rice, dhal and vegetables in the steamer and dashed off to the OP. The steamed vegetables were ready to be 'curried' when I came back in the afternoon with only the seasoning to be done. I would pack it and take it over if I could not locate a wandering ward boy or nurse. I had to do it for each and every meal. Being no workaholic this rigorous schedule did not last long. How could I become a martyr overnight? I bemoaned the good life I led, the bed coffee my mother woke me up with and the delicious food she pampered me with. I missed my father's lectures, heated arguments with my sister ranging from dance versus music to partiality in school, the books that I now had no time to read and the protracted walks on the terrace.

My mother always did everything that needed to be done at home and my father took care of all the work outside the house including getting stationery for us. And now Venkat wanted me to double up as wife, mother, sister, staff nurse and doctor and seemed to think there was wide scope for improvement on most fronts. Little wonder then that we had as many tiffs as we did but none to beat this one.

"How can you come home so late and bang the door in the middle of the night?" I asked, woken up at three in the morning.

"Sister" he yelled impatiently, "you didn't even put the phone back on properly and you are asking me why I am shouting?"

pointing at the telephone which was off the hook. It was the first of the many times he had called me 'sister', hungover from the hospital and not even realized it. I came to a decision. The man was a lost cause, a workaholic who was drugged on surgeries and ward rounds and discharge summaries and OPD. He would not bring home flowers or chocolates anymore as he had during the engagement. If at all he brought anything it would be from the greengrocer I told myself trying to think like him. He was practical, dealt with life and death on a daily if not hourly basis and could hardly be expected to do anything more. If I were a neurosurgeon I would probably not even get the green grocery home I reasoned.

It took a while trying to convince myself but I reconciled to it eventually. I even learned to manage him the way senior sisters managed junior doctors. They put them in their place gently but firmly and went about their own work. I even shifted into the college routine of getting up late and chomping food on the way to the

OP. The house was a mess when I returned, the price of getting up late. One day, I thought ominously, I would drown in wet towels and used clothes and grimy vessels. I wondered how my mother managed all these years with no help from us. How did she cook, get the laundry done, prepare for her theory and practical classes, find the time to raise two children and paint water colors? I saw a halo around her of late and honestly believed that mothers were unrecognized saints.

I was late again. Dr. Acharyulu was still not in but I need not have worried. He was hardly the type to demand why I was late or put me in my place. He usually began talking about his specialized approach of patient management integrating different systems of medicine including allopathy for diagnosis, homeopathy, ayurveda, siddha and magnetotherapy for treatment. He had no commercial interest in the matter he told me, he only took up those cases where conventional methods had failed or if the only other treatment option was surgery. Not that he was against surgery he hastily assured me, at my raised eyebrows, it was necessary in lesions like tumors. I heard over and over again about how he could bring down migraine with his combined approach or how he could cure a wide spectrum of disorders ranging from resistant coughs to poor appetite with his self integrated system of medicine. When I went home on weekends I imitated him between mouthfuls of my mother's fried rice.

The OP waned and waxed. There were three patients. The first one was a little girl with a tooth eruption abscess. I made a nick on the occlusal surface of the first molar encouraging it to erupt through the gum and gave her paracetamol syrup.

The second patient was an old man with a chronic gum infection and he had two lower molars that had completely lost the support of the underlying bone. They moved even if he opened his mouth to speak. But for some reason, he said, he was unable to pull them out himself this time! Could I do it. I obliged him using the extraction forceps. There was hardly any bleeding, so anaemic was he. I give him some of the iron samples the medical reps left with us and he was gone.

The third patient was a middle aged woman who had come to have a lower molar removed. It was grossly decayed, beyond the salvaging stage. It was not going to be an easy extraction either with hardly any crown left to grip the tooth. It had to be elevated till it was out of the socket but if the root stumps became separated I would have no choice but to dig deep with the *Creyer's*. I anaesthetized the area first and then lined up all the instruments I would need. I entered it into the records and began the extraction. After many strenuous minutes the tooth was eased out of it's bony confines. There was a hypercementosed knot at the end of one root and the other root was slender. Had I known it earlier I could have angled the direction of force more appropriately. But the patient was very poor and the x-ray would cost her more than the extraction itself. I worried for a while about the bleeding thinking I would suture soft tissue over the socket to stem the flow but it subsided.

It was a hazy, rainy day. On such a day I would have dreamt of hot coffee or cocoa, a good book, comfortable cushions and music in the background. But now my head swam with images of the tooth I lifted from it's socket. I sighed. A deep sigh it was acknowledging my involvement in dentistry. For all my efforts at making it seem like a hobby it had grown disturbingly long tentacles into my psyche. I now observed people's teeth when I met someone for the first time just as the jeweller looked at your earring or the cloth salesman at your dress. The hospital was an eye opener to me in other ways too. It was a close up of the way health care systems functioned and quite an education about human nature and behaviour. Memories of college were fast losing color and receding into a distant past. It seemed frilly and unreal compared to what I experienced here. I was disillusioned but as Venkat observed there seemed to be no choice to growing up.

When it got hot in summer the corridors gave sanctuary to staff and patients alike from the heat and when it rained even the cows and buffaloes joined the crowd. The bolder fellows nudged the calves closer to the mother so that they would have more space. Pet dogs and cats slept on the kids' beds I knew but felt hurt when I chanced on this spectacle one morning. It was brief, a passing incident, after all everyone would disperse once the shower stopped but somehow it stuck in my head though I tried to move on. As soon as I met Venkat, I narrated it to him expecting that he would be equally appalled and commiserate with me. Instead he said "You are overprotected and need bigger doses of reality. You are in India, remember? I think you need to go to Bihar where they consider cattle part of their family!"

There was an air of unrepentant carelessness. About the way the gardens were maintained, hospital linen was darned or the brickwork repaired. I lamented at the apathy to it all and would wish myself back in time. I think it was these numerous and frank discussions with my alter ego that kept up my sanity. There was no one else to talk to for days on end as Venkat stayed back in hospital doing continuous duties soaking up more passion for neurosurgery.

And suddenly they came. The deer made up for it single handedly. They had a grace about them which relegated everything else to the backdrop. When I first saw them I did not believe my eyes. Deers in the heart of the city? They would appear out of the bushes at the back of our cottage skitting around in small groups and sometimes alone. They became regular visitors and the cottage one of their favorite haunts. One deer became especially friendly and would come every afternoon. If I did not have the morning's *dosa* or *idli* I would give it bread. It came hesitantly in the beginning but became bolder as the weeks passed by. It would walk up to the steps at the back door and take food from my outstretched hand. It lingered for another helping, if it was dosa. Every time I made dosas, I made one extra. I liked the nearness with the deer- the way a wild creature came to me trustingly. The drabness of the hospital atmosphere, the rehabilitation center at the end of the road and the gloom of the mortuary behind it blurred out of focus and I felt good and whole.

I was late again. The little remorse I felt evaporated as there were no patients yet. I stared vacantly into the anteroom of the dental OP where cotton, gauze, and some other odds and ends were kept. Ward boys and nurses walked in and out taking what they needed, sometimes asking permission to enter, sometimes not. Whatever the pace at least the very poor got some treatment done free of cost.

It was my first ward visit. The first patient for the day was 67 years old. She was admitted in hospital for surgery in the abdomen. She also had a toothache and I was called in to examine her. She had an acerbic tongue and seemed to think it was all a conspiracy. She would not open her mouth. She eyed me and the instruments equally suspiciously. I assured her that I would no more than have a look at the tooth that was troubling her. I showed her the mirror and put away the probe. She became even more suspicious, why did I take the trouble to be nice? She had a periodontal abscess and alveolar bone loss. There was no choice but to remove the tooth. She needed oral prophylaxis later to save the others. I also marked the teeth which needed fillings. I would do the extraction after she started antibiotics.

The second patient was a young boy admitted for epileptic fits. He was on phenytoin sodium and his gums were severely affected because of prolonged use of the drug. They were swollen to about thrice their size, inflamed and spongy. They bled easily on probing. He would need gum surgery to bring them back to normal shape and size. I told the nurse to inform me when the neurologist came. I wanted to discuss the drug dosage and the period the child would be on the drug. Was it possible to switch him to another drug while the periodontal therapy was on if not taper it with a multi drug regimen?

I sat in her chair and wrote down both the case sheets in detail. I signed, entered the date and walked down the corridor to the dental OP, in jaunty steps. Who would believe I needed work to feel alive and well? The moody reluctant teenager who habitually dreamt of a beachfront, hammock and music was transformed into a responsible adult who needed the morning's work for the day to feel complete. After a while though, my original state of mind returned and I wanted to go home to rest. Ah, the inconsistencies of human nature.

When there were no patients I doodled on the prescription pad. I wrote about something that had caught my attention that day or about the goals I needed to set or the list of chores waiting for me at home. The third list was usually the longest and I was so overwhelmed at the thought of starting that I never began. I pined for some extraordinary occurrence that would suddenly change my circumstance and I could lead a relaxed life with no household chores. It bothered me that I had never traveled extensively and seemed to be in imminent danger of becoming the proverbial frog in the well. I consoled myself that I was perhaps best suited for astral travel where your spirit wandered over the continents free of travel costs and hassles and returned to your body even as you slept!

On some days there were more medical representatives than patients. One was a man of few words and left soon. The other one wanted me to prescribe his antioxidants as often as I could. It would be of immense benefit to patients he said making tall claims. It was an antioxidant he was promoting, not a panacea for all ills. He talks too much I decided when a young girl walked in. She was diabetic, her last PP sugar 363. She wanted her painful tooth extracted. I advised her to get an x-ray and antibiotics instead. She would be better off with root canal treatment later. She had to see her diabetologist first. She seemed disappointed and relieved in equal measure. Disappointed because the problem was not going to be solved immediately but relieved that the injection was postponed.

I went to see a patient who was a chronic alcoholic. He was readmitted in the de-addiction ward for the third time. A chronic gum infection was among his smaller woes. He also needed an extraction. I told the sister to hurry up with the instruments. They come out of the central autoclave too late I grumbled. I wanted to finish the extraction, go home and shoot with the new camera. On the previous day I had captured a cow on film determined to shoot something live. It was raining and the cow had decided to take shelter in our neighbour's verandah. I plodded over the camera under my umbrella and brought the cow into focus. Used to the many vagaries of human beings it looked in my direction for a while and then decided to ignore me. I got my shot and plodded back already fabricating a story for my sister. I wished I had something to give the cow.

More than anything else, I enjoyed the discomfiture of my sister while I got her into focus. She would smile brightly expecting that I would click soon but I did not. I liked the hazy blur of uncertain outlines just before the subject or scene came into focus and seemed full of potential. The world became amusing afresh from behind the lens. I considered myself a seasoned photographer and took time priming for the shoot. I did not go for potshots. My sister insisted that I was more suited to film subjects with four legs which did not care too much about their facial expression. But Venkat made it clear that all the film could not be used up on four legged subjects.

Another habit I developed after joining hospital was sitting under trees especially those which had a platform around it. It became a fixation as I watched sunlight weave it's way through the intertwined *neem* and *peepal* trees making translucent pools of beaten gold on the fallen leaves and on my clothes. I was instantly transported to my 'abstract' plane. I would have sat there for many hours but for the smell of *sambar* wafting up from the canteen nearby. It reminded me to go home and cook. The owner of the canteen was a superstitious fellow who protected his shop from the evil eye by regularly lighting camphor on an oversized ashgourd, going around his canteen murmuring a fiery mantra and flinging it outside his shop. 'May the eye that casts envy on the place be blinded' his expression seemed to say.

I had an eye on it but only for the *sambar*. Venkat would not let me enter the canteen because he was worried I might become the 'tiffin carrier' type who fetched 'outside' food rather than cook meals at home. So I contented myself with watching the ashgourd spectacle and trudged back to the cottage wondering what to cook. I had decided on cabbage curry and *rasam*. The cabbage was the last piece of frosty greenwhite in the fridge, the rest was plastic. I cooked it on a low flame with a little water. I did not want the high flame to vaporize what was left of it. There was a small ball of tamarind with which I could make a token version of rasam. I hated it from the time it had streaked my plaster cube in college but it was too late to cook *dhal*.

I reached out for the masala box with the seasoning herbs and found that it was empty. How to convince anyone that the hot tamarind water I boiled was rasam and the colorless cabbage was curry, least of all a neurosurgeon? I rummaged around till I found some dessicated coconut. I added a spoonful into the curry and the rest into the rasam making both appear seasoned. Such was the stuff I cooked when I was not in the mood. And when Venkat grumbled, I said 'thank you' as if he was complimenting me signaling that it was end of the culinary discussion and time to move onto other topics. But he was not done.

"How can a neurosurgeon live on food like this?' he would ask giving it a look of utter disdain.

"The dentist may not have saved any lives today but she was in the OP till lunch time and vegetables never appear on the cutting board by themselves,"

I answered. I think my replies got under his skin more than the food. I did not go out of the way to cook delicacies either. Subconsciously I knew that this was one topic that invited discussion. Or else he would wolf it down without a word and leave for hospital. Once I sprinkled powdered pepper liberally on the potato I boil-fried. Proud of the crisp golden brown I packed it with rice and curd and sent it to hospital. Venkat hiccoughed all day and it became the topic of the day in the

OT. Operation theatres are the breeding ground of the hospital rumor mills contrary to the critical and serious image of popular belief. The patient was knocked out from the anesthesia. Surgeons, anesthetists, postgraduate trainees and the OT staff including nurses, technicians and ward boys felt free to exchange gossip nonstop.

When we went home on weekends I regaled my parents and sister with tales about my multifarious menu, the disasters during preparation and the after effects. My mother mollified it by bringing over cooked food and stocking it in the fridge whenever they came to visit us. People had food on their minds most of the time I had figured but resented it because I had to cook every meal. My sister was spirited and innovative about interiors but when it came to cooking she followed my mother's instructions to the letter, the reason why the outcome was predictable, delectable. If my mother told her to add a little rice flour dissolved in water in the end after the vegetables were cooked, she would ask how much and add that much. Not me. I would add maida or soya granules or wheat flour if I could not find the rice flour. And I would even add it before the vegetables were done because I might forget later.

As my culinary failings became legendary, editing while reporting them had become a habit. The stories were liberally garnished with minor untruths to make them more palatable but Venkat never uttered a word there. Besides he was usually always preoccupied. It was surgeries, it was post op, it was wards, it was explanations to attendants, the nurses' change of guard or the sister on night duty getting her instructions right. It could be anything but always pertaining to the hospital. Yet at the cottage he made insightful remarks for someone so disconnected.

"You added the salt too late, it's not mixed into the curry" or " you did not steam the double beans before seasoning and cooked them directly with water" etc. I was astonished that he figured out all my culinary inadequacies so accurately but failed to see that my wilting soul needed watering.

"I am not your slave or servant, I am your wife. Should you not talk to me about other things too?" I demanded.

"How can you say such things?" he would ask sounding genuinely shocked. And before he could protest more or presumably apologize or make me apologize the phone would ring.

The Malayalee sister would screech in a rising pitch, "Ssirrr, the patient is unconscious, ssirrr, are you coming soon?"

And he would jump up and leave without a backward glance or word. Sometimes he would add as an afterthought through the closing door,

"Don't wait for me, it will be late" or "send my dinner at nine o'clock, I have surgery after that. "

He sometimes walked away midsentence and tried to convince me that it was normal for neurosurgeons. I sent the food anyway though I kicked the chairs later. Was there anything else I could do to save lives? I consoled myself that at least it could not get worse and it did. The dates for his theory and practical exams were announced. I felt a panic I had never felt before, not even during my final exams. When was he going to study theory if he went round and round the wards and the OT ? This predicament would continue for another six months even if he got through practicals but flunked theory. I decided to intervene. Venkat would not be pleased of course but I could not take the backseat and watch the proceedings as if it was someone else's life. I asked my sister to collect previous years' question papers from the medical college where she studied and from friends in other colleges. I acknowledged her efforts for once and the results were showing. I had a pile of old question papers. I set to work.

I applied my exam technique of finding out the most important questions and marking them into essays and short notes. I prepared answers for the essay questions and went on to the short notes. I would write them point wise so that he could study it easily, at a glance. Sometimes he would read them and sometimes he would not, always drawn to the operation theatre like a bee to the honey pot. He seemed to need regular doses of flowing adrenalin and emergency surgeries to live on, not food and drink alone. Did he realize how imperative it was for him to get through and get us out of the present existence if it could be called one.

A month before his theory I insisted he take a mock exam. I set the question paper based on my analysis and timed him. After three hours I would grab the paper, I warned him in advance. I corrected the paper and marked it. I gave him twenty six out of fifty and assured him that was because I was liberal with the correction and did not deduct marks for spelling mistakes. Was he expecting that the examiners would do the same? Venkat was livid. He thought I was getting back at him for his comments about my cooking. You would think that at least after this he would not notice that I did not steam the double beans or even if he did, would keep the peace. But no, he took me up on it.

He was the hands-on type who wanted to operate. But I would not give up. I insisted he practice cross-sections of the brain and spinal cord at different levels and color it though he would rather be in the OT dissecting the brain or spine. Neurosurgery was deep in his psyche and I was not surprised when he got up in the middle of the night and reached for the phone.

'Sister' he said urgently, as a sleepy voice murmured 'NICU'.

'Sister, did you tie Natraj's hands to the bed, he thrashes about muttering incoherently and might pull the tube out. Call me again half an hour later. "

Natraj had a head injury, his condition was unstable and he was discouragingly low on the Glasgow coma scale. He needed

71

constant surveillance. Venkat was worried that the sister on duty would sleep through the night, jeopardizing his life if he pulled out the tracheostomy tube without her knowledge. The call was to alert and warn her about falling asleep. Did the neurosurgeon's brain ever rest? I asked about Natraj later and was happy to hear he was shifted to a recovery room from the NICU. Not all of them however were so fortunate. There were patients who were comatose, their brain damaged, their pupils dilated and some who would probably never leave the hospital with their faculties intact or even survive. What a job, I thought sighing. You had to be truly motivated to keep at it. How else could you cope with so much on a daily basis? For a greenhorn, fresh from college I was maturing in other ways too.

I watched the hospital staff going about their duties, reporting to their supervisors, getting work done, airing grievances for redress and also managing a social life of sorts within the hospital. The sincere ones believed that they were doing something worthwhile. That made the difference. One sister would roll bandages all day, another one would pack cotton into gauze and another one would weed out unusable needles. The 'disposable' idea was there of course but it was too expensive to use all the time. The ward boys sorted out the laundry, ladled out food, cleaned the wards and went about a dozen other odd jobs. The trainee sisters would call the senior sister or matron if the attendants got rough or talked rudely. The stern matron would soon remind them that it was all being done voluntarily, for free and that they could leave if they were not satisfied. That stopped them short. Those who had the knack for public relations communicated well and could get jobs done quickly. Such departments ran more efficiently than the others. Staffing was a serious matter in hospitals, I concluded. I found it interesting but little did I know that I would do hospital administration in a few years' time.

I was late again. I dashed out of the house umbrella in the right hand and bag in the left. I dashed right back. I had forgotten my tiffin box on the table. I grabbed it and ran out into the rain this time forgetting the umbrella. Before long I was in the OP dripping wet and hungry. There were no patients yet and probably would not be I thought, given the inclement weather. So I sat down leisurely and started on my *upma*. Kadir walked in a little while later. "I could smell it down the corridor" she said smiling. I took it as a compliment and smiled back my mouth full. She was a friendly ANM in attendance at the dental OP. She always wore red nail polish that stood out for both color and polish without ever getting scratched. She laughed when I vowed to find at least one scratch but I never succeeded however hard I tried. She always came to see what I brought for breakfast and would leave only after she had a look. I offered to part with a tiny portion sometimes but she usually refused though she came unfailingly whenever I opened the box. What a whim. It was easier to stuff myself with toast or idli in the morning but I cooked fancy stuff because I knew Kadir would come to see. I made sphagetti or pasta or stuffed parathas to impress her. Kadir did what Venkat could not do. She thought I was exotic.

Suddenly OP was full. There was a boy with a large hematoma of the right cheek. It was like a small ball you would roll between your fingers and but heavily inflamed. I advised him ibubrufen, chymoral, vitamins and an antibiotic. The next patient was a poor middle aged woman, her clothes torn. She wanted to know whether cavities which were not filled could lead to cancer. What a preposterous idea! Who could have told her such a thing? I answered calmly, "If you don't get the decayed cavity filled, it could deepen further causing a toothache. The tooth may have to be extracted. That is the worst thing that can happen as far as the tooth is concerned, nothing more worrisome than that." She was not convinced. She sat for a while longer trying to see if I had considered all the angles before I spoke. I was patient. I doubted that she could read or write but let her speak anyway and voice the rest of her misgivings. She needed a sympathetic ear among other things.

I sat down to think after she left. Supposing the decayed tooth turned non-vital there would be no acute pain. It would be ignored and the broken edges could irritate and lacerate the tongue or cheek. Over the years it could lead to a chronic ulcer. The ulcer could turn cancerous. There was always a chance, that possibility. Did that mean people should be routinely warned of cancer? Wasn't it more appropriate to say chewing tobacco or some types of *paan* could lead to precancerous lesions? Maybe it was meant to just scare her and make her turn up for the next appointment. Whatever it was I did not like it. It was important for patients to be well informed about all aspects of their health. I remembered the health education camps we conducted in college. It had succeeded even if one person had become enlightened about personal hygiene and health.

Dr. Acharyulu went on extended leave. I managed the OP and the ward visits and signed for him. I was settling down into a life of a kind in the hospital. Venkat was busy as ever but guided me when I called him up for clarifications on drugs or dosages and to get over administrative red tape. In appreciation I cooked a seven course dinner and lit a candle on the dining table. He came late as usual smelling of antiseptic and promptly blew out the candle. "Save it for the power cut," he mumbled grabbing a roti and switching on the tubelight. I became angry and told him I was not going to do it again anyway. After I gave up on such pursuits however he seemed to miss it. Once he took out a crumpled soggy chocolate and a wilted rose from his coat and gave it to me hesitatingly. I thought he was sheepish because his image would change from a 'serious doctor' to 'frivolous young man'. Not so. He got the rose and the chocolate from the medical reps.

Who said you became more mature as you saw life lived out in intense pain and under great duress? Perhaps you only taught yourself to become immune to the feelings it evoked but it was all just as bewildering as before. 'Subdural hematomas, fractured spinal cords and astrocytomas or gliomas' filled the air around us. Critical patients and their equally distraught attendants needed constant attention and yet hospital routine had to go on. At home we were forced to act as if it was normal to have a head injury. Were we becoming insensitive in the name of professionalism? Whenever I voiced such doubts Venkat said, "If doctors concentrated on being sensitive and brought flowers for patients who would take care of surgical procedures ?"

A year later Venkat completed his postgraduation to my intense relief. I resigned from the hospital too. I walked into the dental OP on the last working day. I saw the speckled shaft of sunlight I always saw trailing the chipped wooden table. It seemed dusted with gold. All the other OPs seemed dismal with unadorned 40 watt bulbs dangling from the ceiling or anywhere the electrician found it convenient but the dental OP was luminescent with the sunshine that bathed it and the trees outside. I did another extraction and basked in the familiarity of the place one last time. I was going to miss the dental OP. I was going to miss going there in the morning, miss chatting with Dr. Acharyulu about alternative medicine, miss treating patients and yes, miss the medical representatives and their pep talk, the sister with the red nail polish and the deer.

We moved to Vizag where Venkat went into practice. During post-graduation he had assured me that life would change once it was over. He had even convinced me that he would be home sometimes. 'I am a PG student, what else can you expect?' had been his constant refrain in the earlier years. Now it was, 'I am a practicing neurosurgeon, what else can you expect?' Hospital was ingrained in his spirit and rarely was he free of the smell of antiseptic. But he grumbled that I hardly noticed his absence anymore. All my attention was turned to the little ones who kept me on my toes. My firstborn was a toddler and the second one a baby, a potent combination as any to make you lose weight.

I thought no more of indulging myself on the terrace or abstract thoughts that had earlier occupied my mind. I worried about the consistency of the feed or their thumb sucking as I tiptoed across silently. I had to finish cooking and as many chores as I could while they slept.

Though I was exhausted at the end of the day I realized that there are few joys in this world comparable to those of motherhood. The kids' smiles, their stance during sleep and the complete trust in their eyes when they looked at you, does anything else matter at all, you wonder. They would shriek delightedly while they played with bathwater in the tub and my heart swelled when I rubbed them dry but their crying during the night almost drove me over the edge. Once charmed by the rose however, you must reconcile to the thorn.

Weeks turned into months and months into years. I forgot I had been a dentist once. The kids were at school, the cooking was done and the maid gone for the day. I was alone in the silence of the midmorning lull. Who was I. Where was the girl who dreamt endlessly. Where was the fledgling dentist who had trained for many years. Was the transition so complete that there was no trace left of the girl and the dentist. It began to gnaw me from inside. Could it be that I was bored or had I lost my identity? I was brutally frank with myself as I sat down to think. I took out a paper from the kids' notebook and started writing. The scales fell from my eyes as I wrote. I missed being a professional, husband, kids, home and dog not withstanding. I had to quell my rising frustration or succumb to it.

But where was my saucy spirit. Had housework vanquished it so completely that I had become another housewife at the mercy of everyone else's whims. Why did I feel like a puppet strung up to dance to changing tunes? I was unemployed I told myself though I was busy with any number of chores at home. The years I had spent studying and the few months I had spent working as a dentist had become distant memories. I was probably no different from many other women who qualified professionally but had given it all up after marriage. It boiled down to whether I was going to write myself off with justifications or act before it was too late. I decided to revive my career. But I needed much courage to begin again. It was many years since I qualified.

I was reminded of my father's words. I remembered the time when he had urged me to be enterprising in thought and deed. I thought I knew better as I wandered star struck on the terrace. I had been perfectly content to do nothing for hours on end. But now it was 'do' or stagnate. I recognized it as my wake up call. I had to define my raison d'etre or set myself one till I found it. Then perhaps pondering the stars would become meaningful.

I longed to get back to dentistry but had to act fast before I became discouraged. With every passing hour the task I had set myself seemed more difficult. But who would believe dentistry could rouse passion like this? I tried to think as I would have earlier, as if the present was a warp in time. What would be my next step? I applied to the dental department in the government hospital. They agreed to take me on.

I signed in the register at nine sharp and wore my coat proudly. Earlier I had treated it like a shabby lab apron but now it assumed significance. It made me feel like a doctor again. I found that extractions were the mainstay of treatment. There were more extractions to do than anything else. First the 'new' patient would be given a small slip after diagnosis marking the tooth and the date for extraction. When he returned as 'old' patient on the given date, the tooth was extracted. The patients were seated on benches in the order of their entry and the local anaesthetic injected. A nurse or technician handed the doctor the loaded syringe. After a glance to verify that it was the marked tooth the infiltration for upper teeth or block for lower teeth was given. There was the occasional tearful kid or the hysterical young woman but other patients reassured them.

"It is like an ant biting" they would tell the tearful ones. "I had two extractions done before and I am back for the third, see," pointing at a tooth. That seemed to suffice. They were asked to sit on the dental chairs and the extractions would begin. No more OP once the extractions began. This way we were able to limit the number of extractions per day and spread them over the week. Still you had to be fast. You had to quickly recheck the tooth number even as the forceps was handed to you and extract the tooth in one swift motion. There was not enough time to retract the soft tissue as I was used to.

The grip had to be right the first time and you went into buccal traction without any frills. This was no place for the faint hearted. There were usually at least fifty patients for extraction everyday and sometimes sixty or seventy all to be done by one o'clock. I watched for a couple of days before I started. The staff was organized and would hand over the appropriate forceps for each patient on the three dental chairs, hopping from one chair to the next. I never saw them hand anyone a wrong forceps for extraction. At this rate they could aspire for the 6 sigma like the Bombay tiffinwalas.

I did twenty six extractions on the first day. It was not enough. I held up the staff from lunch by an hour. I was determined to do better the next day. I improved gradually. When I came home in the evening the kids wanted to know the day's score. I was thrilled to be back at work. I felt part of the fraternity though my hand ached and my stomach growled from hunger and exhaustion. I became punctual another first in my delayed career. My speed and efficiency increased over the weeks but I was determined not to make compromises in spite of the rush. I could have asked the patients with broken teeth, the difficult extractions, to come back the next day but did not. Many of them were poor. They would have to forego the morning shift at work and lose the forenoon's pay. The dispensary provided them free medicines but only limited capsules of antibiotics and a few tablets of painkillers.

A few weeks later I got an invitation to attend an aesthetic and cosmetic dentistry lecture given by Dr. Ghatak. He spoke about aesthetics in general and about composites and ceramic work in particular. 'Aesthetics' stuck in my head and I made up my mind to specialize in it by the end of the lecture. It seemed like the most artistic branch of dentistry. I liked the concept of thinking in terms of color and shade. Of matching the shape size and contour of teeth with other attributes of the patient's face and personality. I would go to Bombay and learn aesthetics from him, come what may. I continued to do extractions wondering how I could make it happen.

I was at hazy crossroads and in need of a blueprint for the future. When I looked through the haze I saw an aesthetic clinic and setting it up as my goal. The next thing I needed but could not see was the money. For the aesthetics course and for the clinic. But I was determined that nothing would stop me now that I had begun. I enrolled in a medical transcription course hoping to earn enough for the course fees. The payment was hourly, based on the volume of notes you transcribed. If you did not mind sitting in a chair all day it was ok, even amusing at times. I did not mind. I wanted to earn enough and earn fast. So I listened to American doctors dictating notes about their patients and tried to transcribe it as fast as I could, swallowing my pride. Only the vision of my future clinic kept me going.

Venkat suggested hospital administration as a faster route and I took it up. I had found it interesting earlier and was not averse to studying it in detail. Besides I could do medical transcription from home if I wanted to. I studied for the exams as if my life depended on it. It did. It was far easier to study as a student without the added responsibilities of running a home, getting the kids to do their homework, keeping a busy neurosurgeon from starving and the dog from biting the postman. I was not unduly worried about the results. The question papers were of the standard type. My old exam techniques came to the fore again and I submitted presentable answer sheets. They had impressive flow charts about hospital finance and management techniques. The headings appeared authentic but I cooked up most of the small print.

As soon as I came back after the exams at Vellore I started looking up vacancies for jobs in hospital administration. They seemed well paid but most were nine to eight or nine or nine jobs. Working partime did not seem like an option. With a full time job I would not be able to practise dentistry or spend time with the children. I realized I had strayed too far from esoteric aesthetic dentistry. I decided to work part time in a dental clinic.

I met Dr. Rao in his clinic one morning and asked whether I might assist him. He agreed and I joined the same evening. He was elderly but precise and crisp in his speech and style of work. His son and son-in-law also worked there. They did not seem to mind me much as I kept to the sidelines. Dr Rao's approach was cautious and minimalist. He would drill just enough, grip the tooth just enough and give just the amount of force required for traction during extractions. I learnt one of the most useful techniques of extraction from him though I had done many before. It was patience. He was never in a hurry. Each procedure was done meticulously without a hint of impatience. This was the reason he rarely encountered complications.

A year later I called Dr. Ghatak's clinic in Bombay to confirm that my application was accepted. They wanted me to bring extracted teeth to work on, the air rotor handpiece and diamond burs. I got the kit ready. I begged my parents to come over and take charge of the house and kids while I would be away. I did not know how I was going to fare there or whether the enterprise would bear fruit at all but as I held the ticket to Bombay in my hands I knew I had crossed the first hurdle. I had not let anything stop me from trying.

I believed that there had to be a solution to every problem if we could direct enough energy towards solving it. There were so many seemingly important but actually trivial matters that could drain us out in everyday living leading to paucity of energy. Never did I marvel more at the maxim 'the important should never be at the mercy of the unimportant'.

Bombay

"meteors are the remnants of comets"
Carl Sagan

Bombay means many things to many people. To me it was an awakening. I took to Bombay like a duck to water and felt at home from day one. My monocled view of the world underwent complete change. I had come prepared to work but Bombay galvanized me into action. I felt alive like never before and ready to take on the world. I went to the small balcony of the guest house we were staying and tiptoed across the cracked tiles to the railing. My outstretched hands felt light like wings and I sensed a liberation I had never felt before. The air seemed scented with life though it was probably just fumes from the kitchen downstairs. Something inside me ticked with the pulse of the city.

I was certain Bombay would empower me. Anything seemed possible if you would only try. All my doubts except solvency at the end of the course, fell by the wayside. I psyched myself up thinking that if there was a place that could imbue you with spirit it was this. I would not rest until I gave my ideas concrete shape. Before I left home I had actually worried about jeopardizing my present way of life. Now I wanted to somehow accommodate changes and still keep the wheels of home running too. Bombay was no inert backdrop where events just occurred. It wove itself into the fabric of your life and far too much went on there for anyone to remain reticent and uninvolved.

I felt like running wildly on a grassy slope under a blue sky the wind in my hair. If I put one foot forward I would have toppled headlong into the shabby plywood-topped table nearby but each step seemed to lift me up among the carefree clouds and I was ecstatic. Was it freedom in a new sense or had I just stumbled upon a replacement for gazing at the stars? I had become enthusiastic and felt goodwill and generosity for all. I wondered if this was what touching a chord in eternity meant. I was restless too. Did Bombay do this to everyone who came there.

I found it ironical that earlier when I had time on my hands, the inclination was missing and now when I really wanted to I could hardly spare the time. Oh, how much time I had wasted in my youth, wandering along uninspired. I was so indifferent that I might have walked off the terrace and not known it. Now all at once there were so many things to plan for. I discovered another side to Bombay before long. There was hardly any space in most of the places and yet it could get lonely in the overwhelming crowd if you were not busy enough.

The venue of the workshop was in Worli. We began with introductions and went on to state our expectations from the course. I said I looked forward to catching up because I had been out of touch for quite a while and of course wanted to learn newer techniques. There was no dearth of guidance or materials. I loved working with composite. It seemed like liquid marble and it clicked in my mind that it would be my medium of expression. Others might need canvas or metal to express themselves but I needed composite. Composite was the stuff of my next milestone. I felt great satisfaction as I lifted a cuff of composite off the syringe and bonded it to the tooth. I liked mixing and matching shades to get the exact color of the teeth. I spent many hours dispensing tints and assessing the interplay of different hues as I made it blend with the neighbouring teeth. It was absorbing work.

I had much theory to catch up with, a daunting task. So I sat up at night memorizing the composition of various dental materials, their physical properties, chemical properties and changes during polishing. The faculty were experienced and made sure we got the fundamental technique right. I found that all of them concurred in the basics but each had developed his own individual style and that some finer points were open to debate. I decided I was going to follow Dr. Ghatak's way with composite. He did not truss it around. He handled it with care, a little reverence. It was meant to replace enamel and dentin of the tooth but the polished composite always reminded me of pure streakless marble. Dentistry was as much art as science I concluded. I was glad I chose aesthetic dentistry.

Sneha, Joyce and I shared a room. Velmurugan and Kurien were also from the south and soon we became a group. Just as I loved Bombay on first sight, Sneha hated it. "What a mad rush!" she would exclaim. "How nice Coimbatore is compared to this crazy place." I noticed that in many places the exterior looked dilapidated but the interior was planned. Every square foot mattered. People here were conscious of their heritage even proud of it but in an understated way and would probably not opt to live anywhere else. I felt I could understand why awestruck as I was.

On the way to the workshop the taxi stopped at a signal. A group of beggars came towards the vehicle and asked us for money. We tried to ignore them but they tapped the window relentlessly until we took out our purses. As we discussed how much to give them, one of them pointed towards the hundred rupee note Sneha had exposed as she rummaged in her purse. She was aghast. Who would hand over a hundred for the asking, even if it was Bombay. I was still searching and as usual could not find any money. I usually never found anything I needed in my handbag though it was stuffed. They tried to tell us they had change I think but was not sure.

Though we knew some rudimentary Hindi their style and speed of speech left us stumped. Before long they realized they were wasting their time with us and left giving us looks of utter derision. Perhaps they thought it was wiser to move onto the other vehicles if they wanted to make any money at all that morning. Later I realized I was also angry because they had called me aunty. Was it my *saree* or had I really grown old? I resolved not to wear sarees to work. It seemed to have become ceremonial there and practically no one wore it to work anyway.

We went to the gateway of India. The spacious open arches and columns, the vast breezy waterfront, the fluttering pigeons and the stately hotel Taj across made it my favourite place in Bombay. We watched the sun go down on another day in hectic Mumbai. The sunset made us silent and thoughtful. We were at a turning point of our individual destinies and the poignancy of the moment did not escape us.

A week later we were invited to attend an aesthetic dentistry conference. There were speakers from different parts of the world who spoke about various aspects of practice management. I had worked part time in clinics but had never taken it seriously except to assist promptly so that I was not shown the door. I had never cared to observe even how much was charged for the treatment. The conference was an eye opener. Another appealing aspect was the food. The lunch banquets at the conference were spreads we could not ignore given the skimpy dinners we ate at the guest house. We went to lunch at half past one and stood up to leave at four. It was at the cost of some scientific sessions but by complete mutual consent. I was thrilled by the spirit of Bombay and the banquets at the conference but Sneha was unmoved by both and grumbled about the food. She missed homemade meals and especially despised gravy curries with oil floating on the surface. To be fair it went well with the *rotis* but for the southies rice was a must everyday.

The faculty decided to take us to a disco after a week of uninterrupted theory and practicals. I had second thoughts. I had never been to a disco before. Forget what to wear, should I go at all? Unable to make up my mind I decided to do as the other southies did. Sneha was quite conservative and if she was going then there was no reason for me to stay back I reckoned. The other option of staying back in the dingy room and eating the beaten rice and coriander sauce I brought from home or studying more about composite polishing burs definitely seemed like living life on a lesser scale. After all I was not a teenager in risk of losing my head or being swayed. It would become a 'once upon a time in Bombay' memory after the course was over. It was not as if I was setting a trend and besides the kids were too young to know even if I told them. And I was not going to tell them.

We went. I wore a sequined black top and black jeans hoping I would not stand out in the crowd. Whether it was the dental OP or the disco I always preferred the sidelines. I need not have worried. The interior was almost completely dark. I was stunned at the unbelievable decibel level that struck my ears when we entered. I tried to find out automatically where all the noise came from but failed. The acoustically strategic speakers were impossible to locate. The only light source was an arc that swung mesmerisingly, in ellipses, with resultant sparks on the sequins of the dancers' clothes. My heart beat fast, fast enough to rhyme with the music. It seemed a matter of time before it burst through. But there were people with drinks in their hands, on the sofas and chairs looking around casually, unmoved. Perhaps if I came every week I would look bored too. Some of them from our batch were on the floor dancing with abandon. Not the five of us southies though.

We were dressed for the disco alright but would not budge beyond the railing separating the onlookers from the dancers. It was as if coming over itself was a breakthrough for us and nothing could persuade us to cross the line into the dance floor. We drifted to the restaurant a place where I found my bearings more easily. We ordered *falafel* and iced tea, *channa batora* and *chhass*, salad and steamed vegetables. You could order anything from the Mediterranian to Madras and none of the waiters would bat an eye so used were they to the cosmopolitan crowd. I was certain I would become an incurable foodie if I stayed long enough. Even after we finished our leisurely meal the dancers were dancing still past midnight.

But this was not Vizag or Coimbatore to worry about the time. It was heady Bombay and we were not yet ready to call it a day. We would go to the beach. We took a taxi to the sea front at Worli. The water splashed onto the pavement when the waves were high, in voluminous sprays. Walkers would get wet even without stepping off the pavement into the sand. Sneha said it was ridiculous the way I made everything about Bombay seem good and that people were actually annoyed at getting wet without even stepping onto the sand! The reassuring stone wall separating land from the sea was broad and we sat on it chatting and laughing, late into the night.

We felt like masters of all we surveyed, unaware that we were just another set of admirers Bombay had acquired yet again. When we sauntered down the road looking for a taxi it was three o'clock in the night. How far we had come from our conservative outlook. I liked the Parsi names, the English buildings and Marathi food. In Bombay the ultramodern and the traditional flourished side by side and eastern and western concepts blended seamlessly. There were people from all nooks of India and the world. If you stepped into the road no saying what language or dialect you were going to hear. One rose above all others. It was the spirit of Bombay. True it was impersonal sometimes but anonymity guaranteed freedom.

Many people you met on the local train or on the road were helpful. They would guide you towards your destination and quickly be on their way. They were perhaps new to Mumbai once and now that it was their home they did not resent newcomers. They knew their city was strategic from many points of view. They accepted the floating population. Life was fast. Coping routinely on a daily basis seemed to be an effort. Yet there were many who accomplished a great deal. People who rose in their chosen fields through sheer grit and hard work and of course excellent timing. Moving closer to the heart of the city and acquiring a 2 or 3 BHK seemed to be a sure sign of success.

My mindset had altered considerably and I deplored my previous limited version of living. I wished I had been to Bombay earlier. Things might have been different then. Possibilities seemed endless and opportunities unlimited. Had it not been for my family back in Vizag, I might have considered staying back. I was stunned to realize that. I immersed myself in food an unfailing source of distraction and comfort. I tasted everything at the conference lunches. Each tray or bowl contained something crafted with care but the salad of exotic fruits was the best some of which I had never tasted before. They were arranged with refined aesthetics on crystal platters. There was *bamblimass* at the bottom of a large fruit bowl.

It was synonymous with summer vacations and Chidambaram, my grandparents' place. My grandmother would cut up the *bamblimass* and sundry it to make a fine pickle. We were on the terrace ostensibly to protect it from the crows but ate most of it before it dried. It was years since I had tasted the fruit and there it was, with all the memories it evoked. Bombay made me laugh and cry in turns. I was in a state of flux but managed to find Sneha the *rasam* she missed so much. It was called muligatawny soup.

One evening when we finished early we went to the beach at Chowpatty and to the Haji Ali dargah which was approachable only when the tide was low. Later we went to Crawford market where I was thrilled to see mangoes that too in November. Eight hundred was too much for a dozen though and I left them alone. I could have bought four or even two but as with all major issues with me it was all or none. We had become a thick bunch from the South. Sneha, Joyce, Kurien, Velmurugan and I always went about together. Apart from the southern roots I think the abiding bond among us was the sketchy Hindi we were masters of. I found I could actually use some of the words I had picked up from TV soaps. We called the taxi drivers *bhaiyya* or *bhai saab* depending on their age but asked to see the fare card anyway. This was a far cry from Madras or Vizag where you would never find such a card unless you were willing to prepare one yourself and tuck it into the vehicle's dashboard. Autos had become synonymous with argument.

We listened to Bleaching, Bonding, Crowning, Temporizing and Finance Management at the seminars. Since I had not yet set up a clinic I believed I could implement many of the ideas I picked up there. Dentists already in practice could do it too but making changes in an established practice would be difficult. The qualifying exam was on the last day and though we were all worried about making the grade it did not prevent us from shopping till we dropped. We did everything we told our children not to do. We ate at roadside food stalls and drank sugarcane juice from vendors who could not keep the flies away though they tried sometimes. We giggled among ourselves and smiled at strangers and shopkeepers. We crisscrossed across roads to bargain for something we fancied.

We had scrimped from day one and in the last week no one could keep us from emptying our purses in fashion street or the Bandra shoe market. Joyce had a fetish for shoes. I bought her a pair and for Sneha it was a *kumkum* box in addition to the pickle from Vizag for all of them. We had forged a friendship like no other. There was no professional jealousy, only goodwill. Though we met only a few weeks before Bombay cemented the friendship into an enduring experience. But I missed home.

The green rolling hills, the wide curve of the beach and the little rainbows on the froth as gentle waves lapped up the shore were all conjured up in my mind when I thought of Vizag. But at the forefront were the children playing in the sand with little pails and shovels. I vowed to myself that when I returned I would take the kids to Kailashgiri every week and we would watch the sunrise arm-in-arm as a family. Should Venkat's sunrises always be in the ICU, of the fluorescent type with monitors beeping instead of birds chirping? He had been to Bombay before. He knew what it could do to a first timer. When I returned he listened calmly as I gushed on about living life to scale thinking I would get over it in time. But the spirit of Bombay had taken me firmly in its grip and I would never stop admiring it. The fleeting contact I made with it helped me hold my own later as much as the aesthetic dentistry training.

Practice

"the universe seems neither benign nor hostile, merely
indifferent to the concerns of puny creatures as we"
Carl Sagan

I was an aesthetic dentist now and ready to practice once I set up the
clinic. Soon I promised myself, hunting for premises. No question
of buying anything, I just wanted a place to rent as almost all my
earnings were exhausted in Bombay. I searched far and wide. Either
the rent was too high or there was a dental clinic just opposite the
place or it was on the fourth floor of a building without a lift. It
was almost a year since I had returned from Bombay and I was still
looking. Would my rosy little clinic with palms swaying in front
of glass doors materialize or was I aiming too high on a shoestring
budget that could not be stretched much.

At last I found a place in a good locality near home but the
'advance' was beyond my means. How could I pay up so much,
that too within a week though I could cough up the monthly rent
somehow? I could take a bank loan but still needed a considerable
amount to pay the bank as 'initial money'. I thought about it day and
night. I decided to pledge my jewelry to raise enough for the bank.
I went to the jewel loan section to wait for the assessor. He would
certify that the gold ornaments were indeed 24 karat and could be
safely taken as surety for the loan. After about an hour an unfriendly
old man took the jewelry from me and started to rub them on a black
stone. He examined the dust with magnifying lens and wrote down

some figures on a paper. He left without speaking a single syllable. I collected the cheque after signing in the places indicated and left as fast I could. Banks are supposed to lend but why do they look down on those who need to borrow? Did they only want customers who deposited money in the bank?

Work was on in full swing at the clinic. The carpenter, the plumber and his assistant and four painters were at work. Two of them painted the shutters outside and the other two, the walls inside. Technicians would begin installation of the dental chair after the basic plumbing was in place. I was there all day making suggestions and giving them ideas to cut costs. They seemed surprised at my level of interference but accepted it as unavoidable. I was hard pressed for money and bent on saving every rupee. I checked the day's expenditure as I studied the accounts and started back home only after the workmen left. The office stationery and visiting cards were done. Designing a brochure about the aesthetic work I specialized in was high on my agenda. I wrote and rewrote it as I aligned the written matter and the pictures. I had almost used up loan I got from the bank. If you want work done quickly you have to loosen your purse strings. I was learning a lot since I started work at the clinic. About money and about people.

I was determined not to default on repayment to the bank. That meant I had to work hard, earn enough and run on minimal maintenance. If I had thought long and deep about all these aspects I might not have started at all. It was enough to intimidate many people. I started practice a month later with only one regret. I wished I had started earlier. It was a new interest added to life. In the clinic I liked interacting with people, explaining about good oral hygiene and guiding them during the consultation. I met people of such varied outlooks and attitudes that I was drained at the end of the day.

There was a patient who had a severely decayed molar. Ideally she should have had a root canal done to save her tooth but she did not opt for it. She preferred an extraction. I could only tell her the pros and the cons after explaining the facts. It was her tooth after all and she made the final decision. This was not dental college where we decided what to do and when to do it. This was private practice and the difference did not escape me. Another patient had poor oral hygiene and would require thorough scaling and polishing. She agreed to have it done and after we fixed up an appointment at a convenient time she wanted me to see her son also. What about the black spots on his back teeth?

I sat the little boy on the dental chair telling him it was almost the same as climbing up a sliding board, only there were no steps. He sat down on the chair, tried to slide down a few times and only later let me examine his teeth. He seemed to like the game especially since I refrained from using the mask and gloves. I told his mother that we could put in a pit and fissure sealant over his back teeth. It was another consultation after all but I decided not to charge her for it. Next she asked about her sister's daughter who had rather proclined front teeth.

Building up fractured front teeth, closing spaces between teeth and making composite laminates took chairside time but the results was immediate. If you had enough patience you got the desired outcome. During an appointment I closed a three decade long gap between the front teeth-less than three millimetres but the basis of a new smile. I was so elated with composites that I felt like applauding. I was certain they were the best thing to happen to dentistry.

I had forgotten to pick up the kids from their tuition and drop them at home. And another patient walked in. I told Vijay my assistant to tell her I would be back in ten minutes and bolted out of the door uncaring of the rustling palms. I ran to the tuition center dragged the kids out and took them home fumbling for keys in my bag. I let them in enumerating instructions as I opened the door and ran back to the clinic. I was already twenty minutes late. I hurriedly put my coat back on still panting as I tried to drink water at the same time. I asked Vijay to send the patient in. It was an elderly lady who was more amused than angry. She had a tolerant expression on her face and I told her the truth.

"I know it's very difficult for working women to manage because I have been one so don't worry about the delay," she said and I was grateful that she understood. Her denture was loose. She was worried it would slip as she spoke or ate and even that she might swallow it. Could I tighten it or did she require a new one? That was what she wanted to know. The edges of the teeth were worn out and the supporting acrylic plate was leached to a yellow brown from the usual healthy pink. I told her that she needed a new one without hesitation. I said I would take measurements right away and she could wear her old denture just a little longer till the new one was ready. I checked the sizes of impression trays and chose two. I told Vijay to get the alginate but decided to mix it myself. The last time he mixed it, it would not leave the bowl. I had not yet finished when the phone rang. It was the kids.

They were hungry and did not know how to open the pressure cooker's lid. I had cooked rice and brinjal curry before I left home but had not anticipated that they would be unable to open the pressure cooker. I continued with the impression making troubled. Two minutes later I pulled out the impression trays and checked the shade of her tooth against the acrylic shade guide. I cleaned up the alginate that had inadvertently flown over her lip and chin. We would call her and tell her when to come for her new denture. She was nice but I was not going to unburden the rest of my domestic woes on her. I still had to pour models before I sent it to the lab so I started on the upper which required the denture and told Vijay to do the lower as it was only for checking the bite. I took off my coat warning him to be careful with the models and ran home again.

The little one was at the pressure cooker's weight trying unsuccessfully to yank it off and the elder one had started on the curry minus the rice. There were tears in my eyes when I served them both dinner and

watched them eat. The little one chewed noisily spilling rice on the t
and the elder one objected to the way the younger one clutched the v
glass. They told me about school and tuition. One boy went out to
pani puri in the short five minute break the tuition teacher gave tl
between subjects. That was the highlight of the day.

I put them to bed half an hour later when they finished the .
of the stories. I called Vijay to ask whether he had finished pour
the models. Yes he said, so far so good. That meant he had not
dropped them. I was done for the day I thought wearily putting the
phone down. Vijay called a few minutes later. There was another
patient. His appointment was at six and now it was ten past nine.
The patient must have got the drift of the exchange and took the
phone from him to apologize.

"Doctor, I am very sorry about being so late. It was unavoidable.
Please come and extract the tooth. I have to go out of station
tomorrow. Please. I will wait as long as you want me to," he pleaded.
When I reached the clinic Vijay had the LA injection loaded and
the forceps ready. The premolar was out after a small struggle and
the patient went away thanking me profusely after I had given him
the postop instructions and the prescription. It was almost ten when
we pulled the shutters down. Vijay wanted twenty rupees for the
'sharing' auto. The last bus would be gone by then he claimed. I gave
him a fifty writing off the thirty though I told him to return the
balance the next day. I turned into the road that led home fourth
time in the evening unmindful of the dark. I had an ache in my
arms that bothered me more. The roots of the first premolar were
usually slender and close to the maxillary sinus sometimes abutting
it and retrieval was not easy if the root tips broke. So I had been
very careful while giving traction. I luxated the tooth completely
before pulling it out and was rewarded for my caution when I saw
the unbroken extension of the roots.

I was getting used to action in the clinic. When I entered I liked
to see the clinic lively with people reading or listening to music. I slept

the sleep of the just after the day's work. And yes it was a pleasure to be remunerated for your effort even though it did not make up for the inevitable heartburn on the home front. There was genuine happiness in doing your job well. Your sense of self worth grew. It was joy. It was salvation to know that you were going to live before you grew old and died not just subsist. I observed that on days when I had the do or die attitude there were more patients and on the days I felt like an underdog there were not many. Or was I imagining it?

There was a little girl who needed a root canal for a milk tooth that had to be retained till it's permanent successor was slated for arrival two years later. I wondered how she would react to the injection and the rather drawn out procedure. The endodontist doing the root canal was a little apprehensive too. But the kid turned out to be a wonderful surprise with unexpected maturity. While her parents sat in the waiting room she calmly settled into the dental chair. When the instruments were all lined up and the light was in focus she tilted her head up to help us access the tooth better with complete prescence of mind.

All children were not so cooperative. They were often tearfully anxious about impending pain because of preconditioning. Whenever possible we advised parents not to use the 'injection' word or 'doctor' implying punishment for non-compliance with other issues at home. Negative images formed in tender minds were difficult to banish. The serene little one came back a few days later with a picture for us, a hut with plants around it – straight stems with leaves on either side, classic childhood style and a little girl standing nearby from behind whom the sun rose. I decided to frame the picture and was in a happy frame of mind long after she left.

I saw a patient with teeth that teetered between average size and microdontia. Many of them were missing and the few that remained were just not enough size and function wise. She did not want removable dentures. Apart from making her feel older they were too bulky she grumbled insisting that we give her fixed dentures. It was complicated work with multiple crowns and bridges. The prosthodontist and I started from scratch. We made models of her teeth, articulated them and studied them. We set out to first 'open' her bite (she had a deep bite), called the endodontist to root canal the attrited teeth and then gave her temporary bridges to raise the bite.

Over the next few months we called her in periodically to assess the bite. Almost each time we were forced to make new temporaries as she chewed them to bits including all the fibrous stuff she had not been able to eat so far. Pieces of coconut, hard guavas even muruku. The amount of cement we used was slowly progressing from milligram to the gram category. Luckily she was cooperative in other ways including her staggered payments otherwise I would have to top up my bank loan soon. We were relieved when her bite opened enough to fabricate her permanent ceramic bridges.

We made complete dentures for an elderly patient. There was not much bony ridge by way of support to the denture bases so we focused on retention and stability. He was only concerned about what he could eat. Could he upgrade from the semisolid stuff he was forced to swallow because he was unable to chew solid food? It was the main reason he was going in for dentures he informed us. When we gave him the dentures we watched in alarm as he quickly progressed from milk soaked bread to idli to upma to rice to roti. He wanted to know when he could start on murukku. Why did most denture patients insist on challenging their dentures with muruku?

I was glad when patients paid their fees without bargaining but was sometimes rewarded with nothing less than poetry. There was a patient whose painful molar I removed as it had lost the support of underlying bone. The extraction was routine, hardly the stuff to inspire poetry. But he did not think so. I received a poem many paragraphs long and utterly grateful along with the fees.

There was a patient who was not easy to manage. She was in severe pain and was able to localize it to a particular spot. There was no decay or gum infection or cuspal fracture but the tooth was exquisitely tender and she would jump out of the chair even if I touched it. I made an x-ray to check but found nothing amiss in it either. I asked her about any other neurological symptoms keeping trigeminal neuralgia in mind but there were none. This pain was just a few days old. Nothing particular triggered it off and nothing would make it subside. It hurt nowhere else and there were no other associated symptoms or medical problems. I called an oral surgeon and discussed it with him. He was of the opinion that it could be a cracked tooth syndrome where the microfracture was too narrow to get recorded even on the x-ray film and that extraction might be indicated. I put her on antibiotics and anti-inflammatory pain killers and told her to come for review two days later. The pain must have subsided because she did not turn up as scheduled. Perhaps she even discontinued the antibiotic.

Two weeks later she returned with a large extra oral swelling, almost onto *cellulitis*. This time she was going to need intravenous antibiotics to be followed up with intramuscular or oral doses. Hoping to convince her of the gravity of the situation I told her the infection could spread further if she was irregular with the antibiotic and that she should not neglect appointment schedules. Again however she did not turn up on the day of the appointment. I asked Vijay to call her up and remind her. She replied that she was fine, the pain and the swelling had come down and that she would come the next day. She did not and had me worried. Then an event occurred that made me forget it. I was offered a teaching post as lecturer at the dental college. I would have to restrict clinic timings to the evening but the offer was too tempting to resist. Going back to college seemed like a terrific idea after the long break. It would feel good to be back in the academic fold as faculty.

Teaching

"the laws of nature are the same throughout the cosmos"
Carl Sagan

I joined as lecturer at the dental college. There was green wherever I looked and the open space was wide and welcoming. The outdoor came into the indoor and I felt connected to the elements. I looked at the tall wild grass growing outside the department. Watching a few blades of grass tune in to the wind was fascinating enough but here there was a field full dancing in gleeful abandon. I had assumed that the beauty of the solitary tree was unrivalled in nature but now revised my opinion. The humble grass has great charm. Unlike the fine arts you needed no training to appreciate it. What was the need when it spoke directly to your soul. It was inner peace. Quiet. I felt petty worries lift off my shoulders and dissipate into the wind. This sense of oneness and wellness inherent in communion with nature could really soothe ruffled feelings, well most.

My first lecture was a couple of day later and I had butterflies in my stomach. I had to talk to first year students about essential nutrients vitamins and minerals. Generalizations like "carrots are good for your eyes, calcium for teeth and bones" were not going to help. I took out textbooks of nutrition and biochemistry and started with the chemical composition and kept at it till I got to the symptoms of insufficiency and excess. I wrote and rewrote notes and finally drafted it onto OHP sheets. I had a thick file built up.

I hoped I would not stumble too much or lose the power of speech on the day of the lecture.

I wore a faded checked blue saree to class. It was threadbare handloom but had proved itself many times over for luck, for not letting situations get out of control. I did not want to read out each line from the OHP because the already dry topic would become monotonous. So I rehearsed my lecture many times and even tried out a few jokes. I forgot the jokes in the lecture hall but the lecture itself went on without too many glitches. As soon as I started writing on the board, the chalk slipped from my fingers and when I bent down to retrieve it the OHP sheets came tumbling down. The numbering order was lost. They must have known it was my first lecture.

They asked me to repeat certain sentences when I was fast and I had to look at the OHP sometimes when I lost the thread but towards the end of the lecture I became less diffident. I even dared to ask the class a few questions. They seemed a nice enough bunch of kids and quite sympathetic. They put the attendance register in my hand after I finished and when I came to names I could not pronounce they would stand up and say 'present ma'am'. They said I could just call out the numbers on the roll but I did not want to do that. I thought it was too impersonal for kids just out of school.

They asked me when the next class was and then politely stood up en masse. As I walked out of the class I breathed a huge sigh of relief. It took me a while longer to get into the teaching mode. I went to the library and started studying. I studied like never before and found that the more I studied the more there was to study. I was determined to read as much as possible about the allotted topic and then found that lateral reading helped a lot too. I was amazed at the interrelatedness of seemingly different topics, as I had been in college. The difference was that now I was serious about dentistry. If only I had studied like this in college, I mused wistfully, I might have had gold medals to show my children.

Time was a major constraint now. It was becoming increasingly difficult to juggle home and kids, college work during the day and clinic appointments in the evening. I was exhausted by the end of the week. I would wait for sunday everyday of the week starting from monday.

I sauntered around the campus sometimes to rejuvenate myself. Once while walking slowly under a banyan tree I saw a thin thread like haustorium growing down. I might have missed it had I walked briskly but in my tired slouch I saw it hanging down perilously from the great height of the tree braving many odds like the wind, the crows and careless walkers. It was an insignificant neighbour of other substantial haustoria but went down keeping up its promise of support to the tree.

As I mused on I saw sunlight filtering in through the branches and making golden dapples on everything below it. It felt like music you could see. You heard it when branches heaved and leaves rustled in the wind. A clear blue sky and a green clad mountain with wispy clouds at its peak were the other silent collaborators in this little catch of eternity. I felt immense gratitude for such contemplative moments. They made up for the uneven pace and trivia of everyday life and the drabness and inevitability of it all. I wanted to keep this pleasant relaxation and indolent pensiveness intact. It was nothing less than an energetic character or presence of mind.

I thought of the time when I had not begun my second innings at dentistry. Sunday and monday were the same then. Pictures of a leisurely past crossed my mind. Especially of late evenings when the kids were bathed, fed and played as long as possible before bedtime. After nine I would give them stern looks, lift them up bodily and tuck them into bed amidst loud cries and protests. They would be silent for a while, trying to look through half closed eyes. Then they would plead hunger or thirst or point at the blanket getting caught in their feet. Anything to keep awake. The little one usually fell asleep after a while but the elder one would call me back when

I tiptoed out of the room. "Sing a song," she would insist "or I will not close my eyes." Blackmail I protested but sang anyway. 'We three kings' I began and went off key, then 'mudakarata modakam' and again went off key, the pitch unsustainable. When she finally fell asleep I sat down with the newspaper twenty hours late.

I thought about the clinic. It was cheerful, not impersonal and smelling of antiseptic. There were a few paintings and potted palms but I said the staff went too far when they lit incense in the lab. The other reason it felt like home could be the shady neem tree at the entrance. Did it have much to do with our ancestors being arboreal? When I started I had been warned from many quarters some dental and others non-dental that I should be prepared for a long incubation period. A year later I must have become quite complacent because I was making regular payments to the bank but did not realize how much till I saw a banner on a building across the road.

"Dental clinic" the first line said in red and the second in smaller print, "opening shortly." Competition. I knew how difficult it was to identify the right place, I had gone around enough after all. And I had walked away from obvious good choices for the one reason that there was already a dental clinic in the vicinity. Were'nt they going to do the same then? When Venkat said I needed to grow up I replied that he had grown too jaded to feel anymore. I decided to do something new to take my mind off the matter. Maybe I could learn another language or start a handwriting class. I made up my mind to take up an issue I had shied away right from my college days. Root canals.

I had a long list of reasons why I would not do them. I worried that I could not see enough. About bleeding that prevented me from locating the orifices. About the x-rays. What if they were elongated or shortened. Would the working length be appropriate? And about lateral canals I could not access. Even if all went well I still had to spend quite a while doing the biomechanical preparation while constantly irrigating the canals. And it usually took at least two sittings if not more. I decided it was just what I needed. I enrolled in a workshop on root canals.

Day one:

I was the oldest participant there and thought it was a mistake perhaps. Was it too late to go back to the foreign language or handwriting class?

Day two:

I began working and struggled to correlate the configuration of root canals in the book and the extracted teeth we worked on.

Day three:

I located the orifices of the canals allotted and felt jubilant as I accessed them. It did not last long. Other nimble fingered participants were already into the biomechanical preparation, the next step. But BMP was the same for all the teeth anyway.

It was my first root canal in the clinic. The upper central incisor of a college student was broken by a misjudged cricket ball. The tooth was sensitive and painful because of the exposed pulp tissue. I took a diagnostic x-ray to get started. I asked the patient to sit upright in the chair, positioned the x-ray cone and said 'shoot' to my assistant. I began the access opening while she developed the film. The root canal continued to bleed. The extracted teeth I had practised on were vetted versions hardly exhibiting the copious flow I witnessed in the vital tooth. The bleeding stopped only after all the pulp tissue was extirpated. I started with the working length and progressed incrementally from the smaller files to the larger. I packed the pulp chamber, put in a temporary filling and scheduled to see the patient after a few days. The next time he came I completed the filling of the root canal. As I now obsessed with root canals the reason I began doing them began to fade even though some emotions were unprintable still.

Holland

'all technical civilizations must have a common
language- the rosetta stone of science and maths'
Carl Sagan

We were visiting Holland. Venkat would be in neurosurgery and I at
the dental department as observers. When I emailed them Dr. Stoffel
wrote back to say that I was welcome especially since I was interested
in aesthetic dentistry. I reached the dental school, tandheelkunde,
on a cold November morning. Mingled with the warmth inside was
the familiarity of the old dental chair occupying center stage on the
ground floor. The chair was antique by Dutch standards and hence
on display at the entrance but it was run of the mill stuff in some
parts of India still. It was positioned at an angle to bring out its
salient features including the polished leather headrest and armrests.
The area was subtly lit from above throwing parts of the chair into
enigmatic shadows and highlighting some others. A bureau nearby
housed cements and other dental materials used in earlier times.

I told the receptionist I was from India. He spoke no English and
I no Dutch but he smiled pleasantly and directed me towards the lift.
I rode up to the sixth floor trying to warm my numbed fingers. No
wonder they mechanized so much, what could you do with frozen
digits? The red brick interior and the brightly colored pictures on
the wall were cheerful and cosy after the grey cold outside. There
were doctor's assistants in spotless white walking in and out of the

operatories. They ushered patients in or showed them out with the inimical 'd*a*g' the Dutch word that serves as both hello and farewell.

Dr. Stoffel who had invited me over was a prosthodontist. He was away on a field trip to Hertogenbosch at a peripheral hospital. His matter-of-fact assistant called him up. She was fluent both in Dutch and German but both were Greek to me as I didn't speak a word of either. She also tried speaking very slowly but it did not help. She began again in English, the smattering she was mistress of. She said I could wait in the doctor's room till Dr. Stoffel came back at noon or I could come again the next day. I decided to wait till he came. It seemed a better idea to stay indoors compared to the prospect of trudging back in the cold job undone.

In the meanwhile news spread that there was an observer from India and they offered me cookies and coffee as I waited in the doctor's room. I had walked from the main entrance of the hospital lobby enquiring at the reception desk of each building and frozen stiff when I reached the tandheelkunde. I had only a sweater and overcoat on and felt the cold permeate my bones. My nose ran the minute I stepped out of the heated interior. I needed many wads of tissue to get from one place to another. I had a large handbag with the usual clutter made heavier by documents and xeroxed copies of the invitation letter. I would lug the bag around hardly conscious of it back home but here it seemed too heavy to carry in addition to the overcoat. I tried to appreciate the brave shades of rust on a few trees as I looked out of the window. The chilly grey seemed to monopolize everything. The first thing I did when I entered a place was to look for the heater and stand as close to it as possible. I already longed for the sunny sultry afternoons in Vizag. Couldn't some of the cold from here be traded for the heat there and vice versa?

Dr. Stoffel came an hour later. He was the tallest man I had ever seen towering at least five heads over mine. He spoke English fluently and welcomed me cordially. He introduced me to his colleagues and said I could start from the next day at eight in the morning. He enquired about lunch and told the staff to find me a locker. Other dentists who joined in had many stories to tell about their relatives' trips to India. They wanted to know more about the place I came from. They wanted to know in which part of India was Vizag, how hot it was there and how far it was from the Taj mahal and from Bombay.

I made little excursions into the campus. There were students everywhere I turned and the campus made me feel like one too. The trees were old but the sculptures on pedestals neo-modern, abstract and thought provoking. I went to the post office, the secretariat, the administrative office and the bookstore. I walked as far as my frozen feet would carry me. Venkat instructed me to use euros sparingly. He seemed to be trapped in the colonial mindset still and was bent on making sure that the Europeans would gain nothing more from us by way of direct or indirect revenue.

That weekend we were free to tour Amsterdam. It was the tourist route of windmills, squares, canals and bridges, cheese factories and wooden shoe factories. I watched and listened wide eyed as our guide Robin, short for Rabindranath, drove us around. Robin picked us up at Schiphol and made all the travel arrangements throughout our stay in Europe. We were meeting him for the first time but he took us home to stay till our reservations were confirmed. We were moved by Dutch hospitality as his wife and daughter welcomed us into their home.

Le Klas took my breath away. It was a busy restaurant but everything else about it was leisurely. The building itself was about three hundred years old and there were magnificent potted plants placed where sunlight came through the stained glass windows. The high ceiling was hung with beautiful glass domes and there was pretty delftware on the tables. Windmills dominated the theme. The chocolate Robin ordered was piping hot and the fresh cream so light you could hardly feel it on your tongue. Henry was the other tour guest for the day and a 747 pilot. He was grim and nodded gravely at Robin's lively comments. His replies were grunted in polite monosyllables. Perhaps he had seen more and with more perspective that altitude bestowed upon him. Either that or British understatement. Venkat was moved all right but his usual train of thought was to identify an equivalent place in India that would make it to the international tourist map one day.

And then I heard them. The voices from the next table carried over and I saw an old man and a young one in earnest conversation. The young man spoke emotionally gesticulating rapidly. The old man listened patiently, nodded and spoke occasionally, his voice deep. I was surprised when I caught the general drift of their conversation. They were talking about the universe, the planets, the cosmic scheme of things, the hopelessness of our destinies and the seeming futility of all human endeavor.

"An entire lifetime counts for less than dust in the cosmos," the young one said and "here we are worried about so many trivial things in daily life."

Besides, he claimed "you were underground after the innings no matter what you aspired for or what you accomplished, so what's all the fuss about?"

I did not hear what the old man said but if I could reply I would quote Carl Sagan

"We are the local embodiment of the cosmos grown to self awareness. We have begun to contemplate our origins. Starstuff pondering the stars. Organized assemblages of ten billion billion billion atoms considering the evolution of atoms tracing the long journey by which consciousness arose. Our loyalties are to the species and to the planet. We speak for earth. Our obligation to survive is owed not just to ourselves but also to that cosmos, ancient and vast from which we spring."

Carl Sagan never failed to exalt me. As soon as we reached the hotel room I began unable to keep the excitement from my voice.

"Venkat did you hear those two guys beside us at the La Klas?"

"No."

"They were actually discussing the universe, human destiny and the purpose of life," I added as I tried to remember the rest.

"Really?" said Venkat in a bored voice.

"Aren't you surprised?"

"No"

"What!?"

"They are in a coffee shop on monday morning at eleven instead of at work. Should you take them seriously?"

True they were in a coffee shop on monday morning but they were discussing the universe and the human predicament. They could have discussed the purchasing power of the euro or immigration instead. Should they not be given some credit for thinking lofty thoughts of cosmic proportion?

"Does everyone have to do neurosurgery to prove that they are not lesser mortals?" I queried unwilling to brush it all off so lightly. I added as an afterthought, "did you know that the development of the skull bones and therefore the brain itself was greatly influenced by chewing forces generated by teeth during the evolutionary process?" Ah! one up for dentistry.

"Ok. Shall we eat? I have to get an Asia card, charge it and call my parents. Do you want to speak to the kids or not ?"

That brought me to more immediate matters at hand. I was back at the tandheelkunde the next day. It was a tuesday and a busy one. Patients were shown in and seated on the dental chair. The case sheet and the relevant reports were kept within arm's reach and then the doctor entered. I found this different from India where the doctor sat in OP and the patients lined up to be examined. The Dutch are good at greeting, with or without the 'dag'. Every patient in the OP seemed special and welcome. Dr. Stoffel would introduce me to them telling them that I was from India. They stretched out their hands from the dental chair, mumbled a 'welcome' or 'good morning' and shook hands again while leaving. I liked the informal and cordial atmosphere in the clinics. I think it stemmed from the fact that there was no financial transaction involved anywhere, only paperwork. The state took care of the monetary aspect. Patients were appreciative of the efforts of the doctors. They would bring cakes cookies or tarts baked at home for the doctor and his assistants.

The first patient was an elderly lady of eighty three. She had six implants done to augment retention for her dentures. The implants were loaded a few weeks ago. She complained that the denture base was causing soreness over certain areas especially on the lower jaw. When he examined it there was indeed inflammation in the areas she pointed out. Dr. Stoffel decided to add on a denture liner. He adapted it over the denture base and told her to come for review a week later. She was on her way out happy with the softer feel of the denture. She waved us all goodbye with a bejeweled hand and a genuine smile on her extraordinarily made up face.

The next patient was a middle aged man who complained of orofacial pain. It seemed to originate in the area of the TM Joint but radiated towards the lips. Tooth related causes were ruled out. Dr. Stoffel then referred him to a team comprising a neurologist, a physiotherapist, a rheumatologist and a psychologist. Before he left he was made to practise intraoral and extraoral exercises and trigger point massage. More investigations were ordered and he was scheduled for review after two weeks.

The last patient for the morning needed ear replacement. He had only a small bud in place of the congenitally missing ear and wanted one made up as naturally as possible. The maxillofacial surgeon had put in a titanium prosthesis into the bone to house the artificial ear. It was 'taken up' as confirmed by periodic x-rays and ready to receive the artificial ear.

The technician who specialized in facial prosthesis was called in and he set to work. The acrylic kit he brought contained many tints in different densities. He used the countertop like a drawing board to mix and match shades. I watched fascinated as he blended different acrylic shades until he had a pink close to that of the natural ear. He shaped the outline in wax using the natural ear as guide to do the final finishing. This would be dewaxed in the laboratory and acrylic would take its place.

The patient wore a silver ring in his normal ear. He brought out the other ring from his pocket and asked whether it was possible to loop it through the artificial one. The technician took it, smiled and agreed to try. I thought it was a great idea too. The ring was decoy. It would draw attention away from the artificial ear. The patient was insightful and the technician cooperative. I was sure the prosthesis would come out looking perfectly natural though I would probably be back in India by the time it was fabricated.

I went to the cafeteria when I was hungry but when the print on the food labels became legible I stopped short. I still calculated cost in Indian rupees. Besides Venkat would hardly view the matter as an emergency. Instead he insisted that I have breakfast like him. He systematically polished off toast and chocolate butter, one or two bowls of cereal and milk, duck's eggs and apple juice. He ate a fruit salad and sweet yoghurt and drank two cups of coffee downing the day's calorific requirement in the morning negating the need to carry lunch.

As I sat opposite him I was reminded of a Tenali Rama story. The courtiers were invited to a feast by the king. The royal meal was so heavy that they had to turn down the *paysam* offered in the end at the cost of incurring the king's displeasure. All except Tenali Rama who managed a few spoonsful. "When the king comes the courtiers must make way" he is supposed to have said. Venkat reverted back to his usual two *idlis or dosas* and a cup of coffee for breakfast when we went back to India. In the meanwhile being no match for such flexibility I nibbled at the toast wishing instead for *masala dosa* and *sambar-vada-pongal*. Most of my dreams ended in a plate.

I found that almost all the food was sweet and it was not easy to get spicy food. Diabetes was already rampant in India and I wondered what would happen if we ate the sweetened strawberry and raspberry preserves loaded on toast and tarts. Mustard sauce was the only one that came close to the hot stuff I was used to. I had lunch with other dentists in the doctor's room. They ate their cheese sandwiches and munched green apples contentedly. Everyday. All eyes turned towards my lunch when I took it out. I had brought the remains of the previous night's *naan* and *palak* from an Indian restaurant. I had put it out on the window sill after dinner to refrigerate it overnight. So cold was it.

I broke off a little *naan,* dipped it in *palak* and proceeded to eat when one of them could not contain his curiosity any longer. He asked me what it was. "Indian bread made from wheat flour and cooked in a tandoor oven" I said and "the dark green gravy spinach curry." He could tell it was spicy from the smell and wondered whether it was hot too. I offered him a piece of naan dipped in palak. "Try it" I said breaking off more bits for the others. They loved it. Many of them took a second helping. They wanted the name and location of the restaurant from where I got it. They learnt to say 'naan' and 'palak' as I wrote it down on prescription paper.

The next day onwards not only did I get to watch Dr. Stoffel as he worked with his patients but was also invited to watch the other dentists. How much cordiality a few stimulated taste buds could evoke. Dr. Van der Veer must have heard about the observer who was Indianising the typically Dutch doctor's room and their food habits.

Perhaps he was not too pleased about this development. He was over sixty and had a weather beaten face, the lines of which spoke of many summers and extremely cold winters. When I wished him he was curt and walked by briskly hardly nodding in my direction.

I was determined that he should have a better opinion of me. I went to the operatory where Dr. Van der Veer was scheduled to see his patient. I read through the case sheet before he came. "Sir," I said, conferring instant knighthood on him, "may I watch you do your composite crowns if it is not too much trouble?" He was pleased that I came early, read up the case sheet beforehand and called him 'sir'. He let me watch as observer. This might explain how the British tried to befriend the upper echelon in India by conferring 'sir' on civil servants and professionals.

His patient was a middle aged lady who complained of food impaction between premolars in the upper jaw. He explained how composite crowns would reshape the teeth, making up for wear and tear over the years and prevent food impaction. She was convinced and agreed to have them done. He cleaned, polished and isolated the teeth. He placed the matrix band and wedge in position and started the etching and bonding process. Moisture contamination was unwelcome with composites at any stage more so during bonding. The phone rang and his assistant became undecided whether to answer it or to ignore it. As it rang insistently I offered to assist and gestured that she should attend to the call. Dr. Van der Veer's attitude towards me changed before she came back. He began to talk to me. He discoursed on the 'earlier days' when dentistry was wholesome and disapproved of evidence based work the youngsters seemed set upon. He was experienced by many more years than the age of the dentists who practiced evidence based dentistry he boomed. I smiled but made no comment. I usually saw in black and white and spoke in a corresponding fashion but was learning the inevitability of grey as you grew older.

Dr. Beekman was a legend in his lifetime. He was the same Beekman as in Beekman et al we read about in dental journals. I went to watch when he put in implants for an eighty five year old man. It was troublesome. The mandibular bone was brittle but he went about it with a sure hand. It took him almost an hour and I was surprised when he was sent away with just two painkillers and no antibiotic. "Everything which was not disposable was sterilized, then what is the need for antibiotics?" he asked when I commented on it. He must have been tired at the end of the day but offered to take me on a tour of the college.

There were four dental schools in Holland and about eighty to hundred students joining each year he began as we started on the ground floor. Each floor was dedicated to a particular speciality of dentistry and some of them had phantom heads in the preclinical labs for students to work on. The current project at R&D was on calcium hydroxide coated implants. Dr. Beekman was head of R&D and he was actually using them upstairs in the OP. They had narrowed the gap between research and its application to the same building! They were also culturing bone cells, pulp cells, epithelial cells and fibroblasts to further regenerative techniques. I saw how vital basic research was for the future of dentistry. I realized that the tour was a rare privilege after it ended.

Every doctor working in the orthodontia department wore a brooch shaped like a Hawley's appliance. All of them had 'ortho' written across their white uniform like a slogan. I met a postgraduate student doctor whose name I never learned to pronounce. He was so enthusiastic about his work that I felt enthused too. He used rats' teeth to study tooth movement for his thesis work. I visited the department again on the cleft lip and palate day. Patients who suffered from the condition would be seen jointly by the team treating them. The general surgeon, oral surgeon, ENT surgeon, orthodontist, oral pathologist, speech therapist and psychologist were all assembled around the patient and decisions were made regarding ideal treatment options on the spot. Patients were not made to wait in every department for each consultation.

The library was well stocked and some of the authors were faculty in the college. It was warm inside the library and the smell of freshly baked bread from the canteen wafted in whenever the door opened. I became a frequent visitor to the library. I was now familiar with the layout of the building and walked up and down the corridors as if I belonged there. I even directed visitors to the lift or the cafeteria. But for the cold I was at ease in the dental school. The Dutch were friendly and human emotions including those of dentists, were the same everywhere. We visited Brussels, Paris and Berlin on weekends. Brussels was soothing, Paris stimulating and Berlin depressing.

The old cobbled streets, the sculptures in the square, the end-of-the-street saxophone musician and the cold in the air were typically European. But the people on the street were from Africa, Asia, the Americas or any corner of the globe. As a Tamil song 'dhimthanana, dhimtanana' played in my ears I felt like a citizen of the world where only empathy with your neighbour and the concept of 'live and let live' seemed to matter. I bade farewell to the dentists and their assistants at the tandheelkunde with little gifts I had brought from Vizag. I turned around to look at it one more time as I clicked on the camera. We reached Hoofddorp where Robin lived to begin our journey back to India.

There were hundreds of windmills in Holland and I had seen a few on the way to the tandheelkunde. But the Hoofddorp windmill seemed the prettiest with tulips blooming in a scandalous riot of colour at the window sill of the old brown and grey windmill. Robin and his wife had done all they could to make us comfortable in their home and had even bought us souvenirs of windmill key chains and delftware to give friends in India. It felt like parting from family as we waved them goodbye.

When we reached home I got my mother to cook all my favorite dishes. I made up for lost time and weight within the week. I talked about all that we had seen till my throat was sore. When it came to Parisian pictures I remembered the Kaveri restaurant in the Rue Trudaine with warmth. They had cooked us many savory meals. I was back home but tandheelkunde was in my mind's eye and 'dag' reverberated still in my ears.

A few days later my grandmother passed away. She had been ailing for some time but it was a terrible blow still. Going abroad, watching European dentists work, college, clinic, all my routine work, everything seemed unreal. The only thing that struck me as real was the fragility of life, its uncertainty and the stark truth of death. I became dysfunctional for a while as I thought about her life. She came from a village near Tambaram and settled down in Chidambaram when she married my grandfather, the engineer at the university. She wrote down the prose and devotional poetry her father-in-law dictated and illustrated it. It was a creative period in her life. She was proud of it as it lifted her up among the literary kind. Over the years she gave birth to many children, watched four survive, grow up and get married. And then she watched the grandchildren grow up. And then the great grandchildren. She had grown frail and accepted the inevitability of death but wanted to live as long as she could. She even spoke about her funeral but at other times you could make out 'save me' from her feeble cries. And then one day she breathed her last losing the battle.

I remembered the days of my childhood when summer holidays meant Chidambaram. I remembered the little works of art she created in her spare time. The rabbit shaped purse she spun from nylon, complete with beads for eyes and soft sponge for the inside of the ears, the stuffed puppy she presented me with for keeping my stethoscope and the *kolam* she created with dots. She arranged and rearranged them till she got "Happy Pongal" written in English around the pot and the sugarcanes. I remembered the clicking of crochet needles as she knitted sweaters and the handkerchiefs she embroidered with our initials near the border. I remembered the tamarind seeds she washed and dried for the *pallanguzhi* game. I remembered the way sunlight filtered in through the window as she knotted fragrant jasmine flowers into long cotton threads for us to wear in our hair, in the evening.

I remembered the little nooks we hid in while playing hide and seek, the washing place where an ancient copper boiler stood consuming large quantities of firewood, twigs and old newspapers daily. The clay stove was also lit to heat bath water for the grandchildren. Every time we ran across the back yard my grandmother and aunt would caution us to go slow near the stove. They cut vegetables in the shaded enclosure to cook certain dishes that needed the outdoor smoked flavor.

We collected dried twigs from the garden and lit a fire in the enclosure. We placed bricks around the fire and cooked rice in tiny vessels. We dropped shredded hibiscus into it and stirred it with drumsticks plucked from the tree. We ground salt and chillies on a large stone and scraped it into the rice for seasoning with pebbles. When we forgot to stoke the firewood blowing with 'whoosh' 'whoosh' noises the hollow metal tube made, the fire went out. We started all over again. We decided it was cooked enough when the smoke made our eyes water. We served it to ourselves on banana or *badam* leaves. The game stopped short of putting it into our mouths. The rice had gelled into a sickly green mass by then.

We tried to imitate my grandmother in as many ways as we could, especially cooking and even the way she cleaned her dentures. My sister and I watched her take them out and brush them. We would also try to take our teeth out with the base, like hers. When they did not come out we went to her pouting and demanded an explanation. Everyday. She would patiently reply that hers were artificial. Why would we want dentures like those when we had natural teeth?

At prayer time we ran in once we heard the tinkle of the bell. It signaled the end of the recitation. My grandmother would light the camphor concluding the chant. There were *tulsi* leaves in coconut water and sugar candy for *prasadam* in two little silver bowls. The old silver seemed to have acquired a sterling character of its own with many years of diligent care. Most of the pictures on the wall were blackened with soot from the camphor and there was the comforting smell of old silk and fresh flowers in the prayer room.

My earliest memory was of my grandfather as he went around the garden in the early morning mist. He hummed to himself as he plucked flowers and dropped them into a patched bamboo basket. He went from hibiscus to kanakambaram to rose to champangi and finally the tulsi. He ignored the arali tree which was en route and had lovely white flowers because my grandmother forbade them in the prayer room. He would tuck the flowers into small iron rings which hoisted up and held the heavily framed pictures on the walls.

I stretched out my pudgy fingers for prasadam, awaited eagerly from the beginning of the prayer. My grandmother would check for the *namam* on each forehead and then give us the prasadam. It was the sign that we had bathed in the morning and it was applied by my grandfather, a minor ceremony by itself. It began when he took out a rosewood box from the shelf in the puja room and sat down in the passage outside where the lighting was better. The box had two chambers with sliding lids. One was for the red *kumkum* and the other for white chalk and between them was a long niche that housed the silver stick used to draw the namam.

He would take out the white chalk first, wet it and rub it into his palm to make a paste. This was for the outer lines which rose from the eyebrows and disappeared into the hairline. He would then make a paste with the red kumkum, in a smaller quantity. He drew it up on the silver stick and centered it between the two white lines. He then pressed it gently into the middle of the forehead completing the namam. I can still feel the metallic slide of silver on my forehead and the gentleness of his bent fingers. He did it for all the impatient children waiting to run out and play.

One morning I was in the garden plucking gooseberries. I threw them into the well to hear the 'thwack' they made in the water at different velocities. I had no bath and no namam but decided to get the sweet prasadam anyway. I thought my grandfather and god would not mind but was not sure about my grandmother. She was particular. I went in and stretched out my hand confidently as she began distributing the prasadam. I rushed out and ate it in a hurry lest I got caught red handed. I did not but unexpectedly it began weighing on my mind. I considered going to my grandmother and telling her the truth but gave up the idea. Instead I resolved never to do it again. The familiar chant of verses repeated everyday, the fragrance of sandalwood mingled with leisurely mists of *sambrani* drifting by, the promise of another day in the garden, playing till it grew dark in the evening, a noisy dinner then verse reading by one uncle and storytelling by another, competing to entertain us and an aunt to referee it all. What happiness!

"Let us see who finishes first today," they would say at the start of dinner and a fierce contest would ensue to decide the winner as we stuffed rice and curry by the fistful into our mouths. It was the same everyday but there was no question of getting bored. We looked forward to each day as only six and seven year olds can, on vacation with their grandparents. It was too simple to dissect for psychoanalysis. It was the very joy of living. I doubted it would ever be experienced again in the same intensity no matter what was acquired or achieved. It was childhood at its best.

My grandparents remained in our memories but what of them. How could so many decades of 'being' be washed away by 'no more' one day. If it was the *'maya'* that spiritualists said it was, could it be so elaborate? Or was I disillusioned because I was forced to acknowledge my own fading away too. We are born for a higher purpose we tell ourselves trying to grasp at the elusive 'purpose'. Was it going to dawn on me because I mused on it sometimes at times like these.

Epilogue

I was back at the clinic. A vivacious nineteen year old waited to see me. She wanted to be a reporter and her interview was at eight o' clock the next morning. She showed me the gap between her two front teeth because of which she hesitated to smile, even speak freely. Could I do something about it?

'Yes', I said, in about an hour she would walk out with a new smile. I would close the gap by sculpt-bonding composite laminates over the two teeth. I added composite incrementally assessing symmetry on both sides as I turned the incisal angles in. If the canines were the cornerstone of the smile the central incisors were the frontal archways. I was happy to see her smiling when she left. A little later I was on my way home having reminded Venkat not to be late as usual. It was the little one's birthday and we were having a small get together. I went about the preparations trying to convince the elder one that the cut of her dress was definitely more stylish, absolutely current.

The thoughtful melancholy of the previous weeks had not yet left me entirely in spite of getting back to the routine. Renewing yourself in as many ways as you could seemed to be the way. Recognizing the precious tenure of our lives makes our experiences enriching and our little enterprises cherishable.

Suja Ravilla Ramana

Later in the evening, the composite laminates were still pleasantly etched in my mind's eye and doubts about the 'purpose' seem to have evaporated into the dark of night as I walked on the terrace the stars shining down.

Acknowledgements

Thanks to my grandparents Vatsala and Anumarla Venkatakrishnan for making my childhood a joyous one. Thanks to my parents Nilamangai and Ravilla Bojji Duraiswamy for their faith in me. All parents must believe in their offspring. Thanks to Dr. Ann Druyan for her encouragement. Carl Sagan will always be an abiding bond.

Thanks to my uncles Dr. A. Gopal and Dr. A. Govindan for telling me I could write though I never believed them. Thanks to my aunt Mrs. G. Sridevi for making my summer holidays worth writing about. Thanks to my sister Dr. Sudha Kiran for discerning minor and major flaws in the draft and for not agreeing with me on certain details in spite of my pointed resistance. It is a prerogative of younger sisters. Thanks to my husband Dr. P. V. Ramana for going over medical details and help with the e-formatting. Neurosurgeons know more. Thanks to my daughters Trilokhya and Sanjana for accepting my apology. There is not enough about them.

Thanks to my teachers in college for their memorable classes and their tolerance. Thanks to Dr. R. Ravi for doing the first editing and convincing me it was worth publishing. Thanks to Dr. Cibi Mammen for help with the sequencing of events during the college years. We agreed on everything except who made better plaster cubes. Thanks to Dr. C S. Prasad for the initial inspiration and to Dr. K. Sridevi and Dr. Sunita Ravi for help with the dental curriculum. Thanks to Dr. Kris Ramamurthy for correcting the spelling mistakes in Dutch. Thanks to my assistants at the clinic Suguna, Tara and Nagamani for patiently tolerating my erratic bouts of typing and keeping me hydrated with tender coconut water.

Thanks to my patients for reinforcing my belief in the profession and people. Thanks to Dr. Arun Tiwari for telling me that whatever I wrote I would want to rewrite it after some time. I wonder whether I should have waited a little longer before submitting the proof online.

Thanks to Michelle Page, Faye Bacus, Ann Ardon and the designers at Trafford for their thorough but friendly professionalism. They managed to make me do the corrections cheerfully.